HANDY REFERENCE

Icons in Quicken

A summary of the main icons on the iconbar in Quicken is given here for your reference.

 Click on this icon to open the register of the account that you were last working in.

 Click on this icon to open the Financial Calendar. This feature makes tracking and planning your transactions easier.

 Click on this icon to access the Accounts List, which holds information about all the accounts in that particular file.

 Click on this icon to open the Create Graph window. Graphs make it easy for you to oversee trends in your finances.

 Click on this icon to open the Write Cheques window. This feature will save you time and effort in preparing cheques.

 Click on this icon to open the Create Report window. Reports provide a useful way to analyse your financial data.

Shortcut keys in Quicken

These are some of the main keyboard shortcuts that will save you time when using Quicken.

Help	**F1**	Cut	**Shift+Del**
Go to register	**Ctrl+R**	Copy	**Ctrl+Ins**
Display Account List	**Ctrl+A**	Paste	**Shift+Ins**
Go to Financial Calendar	**Ctrl+J**	Undo	**Alt+Backspace**
Go to Write Cheques	**Ctrl+W**	Edit	**Ctrl+E**
Go to Portfolio View	**Ctrl+U**	Delete	**Ctrl+D**
Go to View Loans	**Ctrl+H**	QuickZoom a report amount	**Ctrl+Z**
Display Category & Transfer List	**Ctrl+C**	Open a File	**Ctrl+O**
Display Class List	**Ctrl+L**	Back up a File	**Ctrl+B**
Display Security List	**Ctrl+Y**	Print List	**Ctrl+P**

ABOUT THE SERIES

In easy steps series is developed for time-sensitive people who want results fast. It is designed for quick, easy and effortless learning.

By using the best authors in the field, and with our experience in writing computer training materials, this series is ideal for today's computer users. It explains the essentials simply, concisely and clearly - without the unnecessary verbal blurb. We strive to ensure that each book is technically superior, effective for easy learning and offers the best value.

Learn the essentials **in easy steps** - accept no substitutes!

Titles in the series include:

Title	Author	ISBN
Windows 3.1	Harshad Kotecha	1-874029-18-0
Windows for Workgroups 3.11	Harshad Kotecha	1-874029-12-1
Windows 95	Harshad Kotecha	1-874029-28-8
Word 6	Scott Basham	1-874029-16-4
Excel 5	Roy Roach	1-874029-15-6
Office 95	Stephen Copestake	1-874029-37-7
WordPerfect 6	Kate Stewart	1-874029-11-3
Internet UK	Andy Holyer	1-874029-31-8
CompuServe UK	John Clare	1-874029-33-4
CorelDraw	Stephen Copestake	1-874029-32-6
PageMaker 5	Scott Basham	1-874029-19-9
PageMaker	Scott Basham	1-874029-35-0
Quicken UK	John Sumner	1-874029-30-X

To order or for details on forthcoming titles ask your bookseller or contact Computer Step on 01926 817999.

QUICKEN UK
in easy steps

John Sumner

COMPUTER
STEP

In easy steps is an imprint of Computer Step
5c Southfield Road, Southam
Warwickshire CV33 OJH England
☎01926 817999

First published 1996
Copyright © 1995 by Computer Step

Notice of Liability

Every effort has been made to ensure that this book contains accurate
and current information. However, Computer Step and the author
shall not be liable for any loss or damage suffered by readers as a
result of any information contained herein.

Trademarks

Quicken® is a registered trademark of Intuit Inc., Windows™ is a
trademark of Microsoft Corporation. All other trademarks are
acknowledged as belonging to their respective companies.

For all sales and volume discounts please contact Computer Step on
Tel: 01926 817999.

For translation rights, reprinting rights and export orders write to the
address above or Fax: (+44) 1926 817005.

Printed and bound in England

ISBN 1 874029 30 X

Contents

1. First Steps 7

Introduction.. 8
Starting Quicken 9
New User Setup 10
Quicken's Iconbar 14
QCards 17
Quicken's Quick Keys 18
Quicken's QuickFill 20
Looking for Help? 22

2. Quicken Accounts.............................. 23

Adding a New Account 24
Deleting an Account 27
Adding a Category 28
Splitting a Category 29
Deleting a Category 30
Recategorising 31
Adding a Class 32
Transferring between Accounts 33
Quicken Colours 34

3. Entering Transactions 35

Registers 36
Adding a Transaction 37
Configuring the Register 38
Paying Bills 40
Register Reports 41
Memorising Transactions.............................. 42
Deleting Transactions 44
Voiding Transactions 45
Finding a Transaction 46
Finding a Transfer 47
Find and Replace 48

4. Financial Calendar 49

The Financial Calendar 50
Scheduled Transactions 52
Editing Scheduled Transactions 55
Deleting Scheduled Transactions 56
Paying Bills in Advance 57
Billminder 58
Reminders 59
Calendar Notes 60

5. Cheques & Reports 61

Writing Cheques 62
Cheque Options 63
Cheque Printer Setup 64
Printing Cheques 66
Reports 67
Customising Reports 68
Report Options 69
Report Printer Setup 70
Printing Reports 71
Memorising Reports 72

6. Using Graphs 73

Creating Graphs 74
Graph Options 75
Budget Graphs 76
QuickZoom Graphs 77
Investment Graphs 78
Income and Expense Graphs 80
Net Worth Graphs 81
Customising Graphs 82
Printing Graphs 83
Memorising Graphs 84
Snapshots 85

Customising the Snapshots Page 86
Customising Individual Snapshots 87
Adding New Snapshot Pages 88

7. Reconciling Accounts 89

Balancing Accounts 90
Reconciling Accounts 91
Reconciling a Bank Statement 92
Reconciling Unit Trust Accounts 95
Reconciling Investment Accounts 96
Reconciling a Credit Card Statement 98
Updating Cash/Share Balances 100

8. Budgeting & Loans 101

Budgets and Targets 102
The Budget window 103
Manually Entering Budget Figures 104
Entering Existing Budget Figures 105
Tidying up the Budget window 106
Moving around the Budget window 108
Using the Progress Bar 109
Savings Goals 110
Setting up a Loan 112
The View Loans Window 113
Entering Loan Details 114
Paying Loans 116

9. Financial Planners 117

Financial Planners 118
Planning your Savings Investment 119
Planning your Loan 120
Planning College Fees 122
Planning for your Retirement 123
Planning a Remortgage 124

10. Shares & Investments 125

Adding an Investment Account 126
Setting up Securities 128
Setting up Security Types 129
Setting up Investment Goals 130
Setting up Security Balances 132
The Investment Account Register 133
Buying 134
Selling 135
The Portfolio View window 136

11. File Functions 139

Adding a New File 140
Opening a File 141
Deleting a File 142
Backing up Files 143
Restoring Backed up Files 144
Setting up Passwords 145
Copying Details to the Next Year 146

12. Miscellaneous Features 147

Currency 148
Selecting International Preferences 150
Using the Calculator 151
Tracking VAT 152
Changing VAT Rates 154

Index 155

First Steps

This chapter will get you started with Quicken. It covers the initial settings you will need to make before you can start proper.

Covers

Introduction 8

Starting Quicken 9

New User Setup 10

Quicken's Iconbar 14

Qcards 17

Quicken's Quick Keys 18

Quicken's QuickFill.. 20

Looking for Help? 22

Introduction

Everyone worries about their financial plight; Am I overdrawn? Am I going into debt? Keeping track of your money can be a real headache. Quicken can't solve any of your money problems but it can help tremendously in how you organise your financial life.

What can Quicken do for you?

Quicken can handle as many of your accounts as you wish; accounts for savings, credit cards, investments and many others. Once you have entered these into your own data file it's easy for you to manage your financial affairs.

Some of the things you can do are:

- Produce graphs and reports of all of your transactions, which you can then customise.

- Create a single report or graph, containing details of all your accounts, making it easy to keep an eye on your net worth.

- Keep a single list of expense and income categories for your accounts.

- Plan your future finances, such as saving for your retirement, your children's school fees or a new car.

- Easily move money from one of your accounts to another.

Using Quicken can also save you a lot of time when printing cheques, reconciling your accounts and will even alert you to any future bills you have to pay.

Don't worry if you have no previous experience of maintaining your finances as Quicken is very easy to work with, using no accounting jargon, and it works in a logical way.

Starting Quicken

Switch on your PC and log into Windows as normal. If Quicken has been installed, the Quicken icon will appear in the Program Manager window.

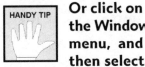

HANDY TIP

Or click on the Window menu, and then select the Quicken option.

Double-click on the Quicken icon.

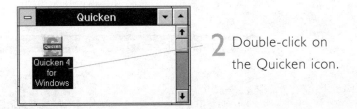

The Quicken desktop will now appear.

2 Double-click on the Quicken icon.

If you are using Windows 95 this process will be slightly different.

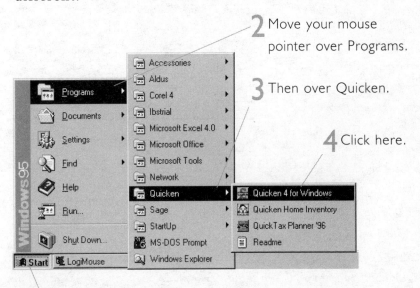

2 Move your mouse pointer over Programs.

3 Then over Quicken.

4 Click here.

Click on the Start button.

New User Setup

If this is the first time Quicken is being used, or if no account details have previously been entered, you will initially be confronted with the New User Setup window.

You will be taken step by step through the initial setup procedure, that you'll have to follow, to create your first account.

The New User Setup windows must be completed before you are allowed to start working with Quicken.

This panel indicates which section of the User Setup group you are currently in. Once a section is finished it is ticked off.

Panel containing information about each section.

Click for help.

Click to proceed to the next window.

...contd

Setting up a deposit account

REMEMBER

You will need to have your account details with you when opening an account.

I Click on the Next button in both the Tutorials window and in the Current Account windows.

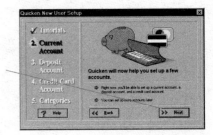

2 Click here.

3 Enter the account name, and then click on the Next button.

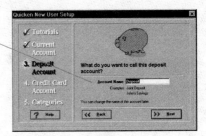

4 The next panel will ask you if you have your last bank statement for this account. If you click on the No button, you will go directly to the track VAT panel. If you click on Yes, you will go into the statement date panel.

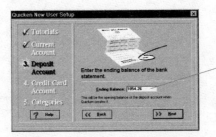

5 In the next two panels enter the last date and the balance from your bank statement.

...contd

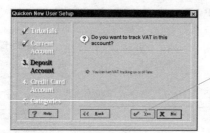

6 If you are using Quicken for business use, the next option asks you if you want to record or track VAT. Click on the next button if you do.

At the end of defining each account, Quicken will display dates and starting figures for you to confirm.

7 Next define a currency for your account. Normally this will be the Pound, but if you have a foreign account you can select another currency from the list.

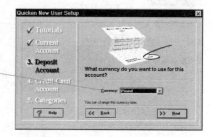

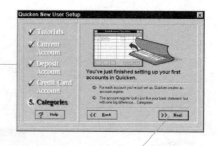

8 Confirm the account details by clicking on the Next button, otherwise use the Back button to amend your details.

You will then be asked if you want to set up a credit card account. Click on the Yes button if you do or click on the No button to display this window.

Click here to start the categories panels.

...contd

Selecting your categories

Quicken's Categories feature lets you group various types of income and outgoings you incur, so that you can easily see how your money is being spent or received.

Quicken provides a list to choose from, or alternatively, you can define your own.

HANDY TIP **Avoid creating a large number of categories initially. Start with a small number of categories to cover general groups and add more, as required.**

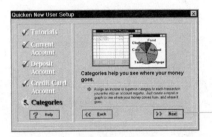

Click on the Next button.

2 To save you typing all your required categories from scratch, select one of the groups on offer and then add or adjust, as necessary.

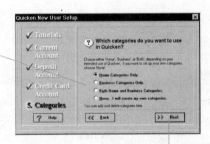

3 Click here.

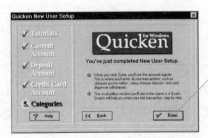

4 Finally, from the last window, click on the Done button to finish the New User Setup. You can now start working with Quicken.

Quicken's Iconbar

The main iconbar can be configured to suit your own requirements. It is advisable to remove icons from the bar which you do not expect to use. They can be replaced and others added later, as required. The graphics on the buttons can also be changed to reflect your own needs.

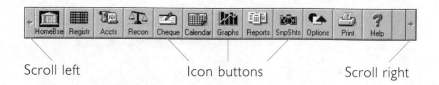

Scroll left   Icon buttons   Scroll right

Customising your iconbar

From the main iconbar, click the Options icon and then the Iconbar button.

HANDY TIP

Only include the icon buttons that will be used frequently.

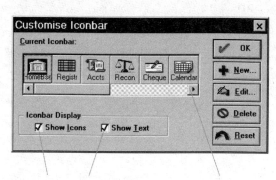

Selecting the Iconbar Display options produces buttons with either graphics only or text only, or both. Unchecking both options removes the iconbar from the display.

Scroll along to view the other icons present on your Iconbar.

...contd

Adding a new icon to the iconbar

1 From the Customise Iconbar window, click on the New button.

2 Click on the required action from the list.

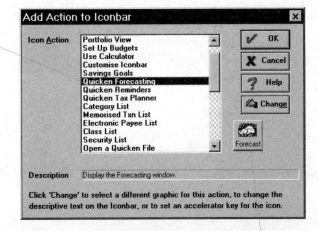

3 Click OK to add your selection to the iconbar.

Quicken shows you what the icon will look like on the iconbar.

Deleting an icon from the iconbar

1 From the Customise Iconbar window, click on the icon to be deleted.

2 Click on the Delete button.

3 Click on OK to remove the icon from the Iconbar.

HANDY TIP

You can also edit the icons when first adding them to the iconbar - when in the Add Action to Iconbar window click on the Change button to display the Change Iconbar Item window.

Editing an icon

This option lets you change an icon button, or the way it is displayed. You can also change the wording for it and define SpeedKeys for quick selection.

1 From the Customise Iconbar window, click on the icon to be edited.

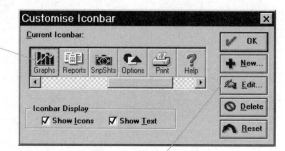

2 Click on the Edit button.

3 In the Edit Action on Iconbar window, click on the change icon.

4 Select the new graphic for the icon.

5 You can change the wording for the button, if you want.

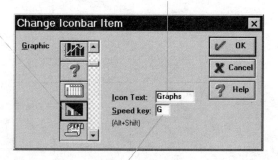

6 You can also assign a Speed Key letter to your icon. By pressing this letter together with the Alt+Shift keys you will automatically start the option.

7 Click OK, when you have finished.

QCards

QCards are small windows which can be displayed each time certain entries have to be made. They act as mini-help screens, containing instructions about what type of action you need to take and what details you need to enter.

Turning QCards On and Off

For the beginner Qcards are a real help, but after you have used Quicken for some time they can begin to get in the way, and are best turned off.

From the Help menu, click on the Show Qcards option, if it is not already selected (ticked).

Qcards will now be activated every time you move your mouse pointer over an account field, to give you some guidance.

Click here to turn off this Qcard.

Click OK to turn off Qcards for this window.

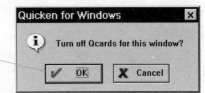

Quicken's Quick Keys

The Quicken program has many Quick Keys, which once remembered, can make the program much easier and quicker to use. Listed below are the Quick Keys used in addition to those normally used in most Windows programs.

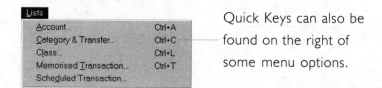

Quick Keys can also be found on the right of some menu options.

The following are basically used for moving around the various program windows and for quick inserts into fields. More Quick Keys can be found in the Handy Reference section, at the front of the book.

Special Keys

- (Minus key)	Decrease Date or Cheque Number
+ (Plus key)	Increase Date or Cheque Number
Ctrl + Z	QuickZoom a Report Amount
1st Letter of Item	Select an item in a drop-down list

Dates

t or T	Today
m or M	First day of Month
h or H	Last day of Month
y or Y	First day of Year
r or R	Last day of Year

Moving around in a window

Tab	Next Field or Column
Shift+Tab	Previous Field or Column
Home	Beginning of Field
Home+Home	First Field in Transaction or Window, or First Report Row
Home+Home+Home	First Transaction in Window
Home+Home+Home+Home	First Transaction in Register
Ctrl+Home	First Transaction or Upper Left Corner of Report
End	End of Field
End+End	Last Field in Transaction or Window, or Last Report Row
End+End+End	Last Transaction in Window
End+End+End+End	Last Transaction in Register
Ctrl+End	Last Transaction or Lower Right Corner of Report
PageDn	Next Window or Cheque
PageUp	Previous Window or Cheque
Ctrl+PageDn	Next Month
Ctrl+PageUp	Previous Month
Up Arrow	Move Up one Row
Down Arrow	Move Down one Row

Quicken's QuickFill

QuickFill is Quicken's automatic data entry feature. For example, when activated you only need to type in the first few characters of a category before Quicken fills in the full category entry. Using QuickFill can save considerable time where repeated entries are made, or expected.

However, if not set up properly to reflect your own needs, it can be a nuisance. Although you can change the QuickFill options at any time, it is advisable to set up this feature before you start using Quicken.

From the main iconbar, click on the Options icon, and then click on either the Register or Write Cheques buttons.

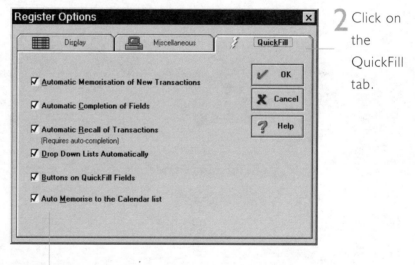

2 Click on the QuickFill tab.

Quicken will have already selected all of these options by default.

3 To turn off an option click the checkbox so that the box is clear, and click on the option if you want to activate it again. An explanation of each option is given on the opposite page.

4 Click OK to finish.

☑ **A**utomatic Memorisation of New Transactions

Activate this option if you want the program to memorise new transactions entered into the register (except Investments) - see Chapter 3.

☑ Automatic **C**ompletion of Fields

With this option activated, Quicken will automatically complete the entry of fields based on previous entries.

☑ Automatic **R**ecall of Transactions
(Requires auto-completion)

With this option selected you can enter a transaction by typing just the first few characters followed by the Tab key. The program will complete rest of the details for you.

☑ **D**rop Down Lists Automatically

When this option is activated, Quicken automatically displays a list of choices when the cursor is in certain fields in the register.

☑ **B**uttons on QuickFill Fields

With this option selected, the program will display a button on fields where Quickfill can be used.

☑ Auto **M**emorise to the Calendar list

This option automatically adds transactions to the Financial Calendars transaction list.

Looking for Help?

For the beginner, tackling Quicken can look like an ominous task but help is always close at hand. Quicken provides a very good onscreen help system which can be activated in several different ways.

When calling for help, Quicken will automatically bring up the relevant help dialogue box for the current task or function that you are working on.

 For quick access to the Help windows press F1.

From the Help menu, click on the Quicken Help option, or more easily from the main iconbar click on the Help icon.

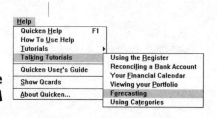

 If you have a CD-ROM version of Quicken, Talking Tutorials are also available. These provide multimedia training on some aspects of Quicken.

Click here to access a table of contents of Help topics.

Click on here if you want to get help for a specific word or topic.

Click on here to access the glossary where you can find explanations of the terms used in Quicken.

Click on words underlined with a dotted line to bring up its popup definition.

Click on any topic which is underlined with a solid line to access a window which will give you more information about that topic.

CHAPTER TWO

Quicken Accounts

Here we will look at Quicken accounts, categories and classes.

You can have up to 64 accounts in each Quicken file. One Quicken file can be used for business use and one for home use, or you can combine the two into one file.

Quicken's categories and classes help to organise transactions so that useful information can be extracted from the system at a later stage.

Covers

Adding a New Account 24

Deleting an Account 27

Adding a Category 28

Splitting a Category 29

Deleting a Category 30

Recategorising 31

Adding a Class 32

Transferring between Accounts 33

Quicken Colours 34

Adding a New Account

During any financial year there may be occasions when you need to open a new account. This may be a bank, building society, investment account, etc., and each must be a separate account in Quicken.

To explain this procedure we will create a deposit account.

HANDY TIP

Alternatively open an account by selecting the New button in the Accounts List window.

1 From the Activities menu, click on the Create New Account option.

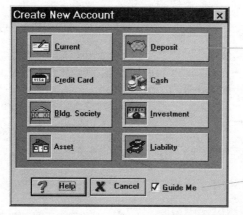

2 Click the account required - in this case Deposit.

Click to be guided by Quicken.

3 Enter the account name.

4 Enter the name of your bank or account number.

5 Click here to continue.

...contd

6 You will be asked if you know either the account opening
balance, or the balance from your last statement.

If you answer 'No', Quicken will set the account with a £0.00 (zero) opening balance.

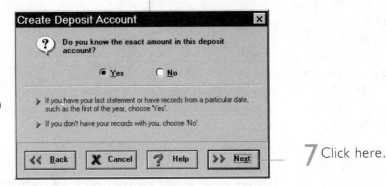

7 Click here.

8 Enter the opening or last statement date. You can click
on the calendar button to select the date from there.

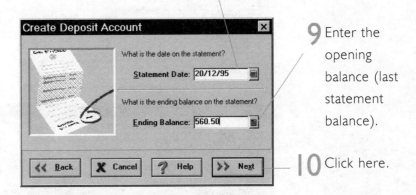

9 Enter the
opening
balance (last
statement
balance).

10 Click here.

If you are in business, and are VAT registered answer Yes, otherwise answer No.

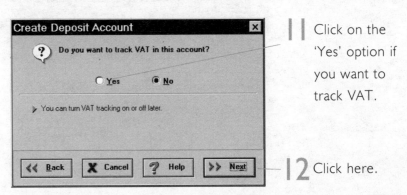

11 Click on the
'Yes' option if
you want to
track VAT.

12 Click here.

REMEMBER

Normally the account currency will be the Pound, but if you have bank accounts or investments in other currencies you can select the appropriate one from the drop-down list.

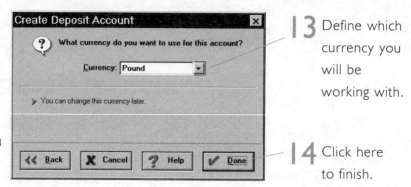

13 Define which currency you will be working with.

14 Click here to finish.

When complete, Quicken will display the account register.

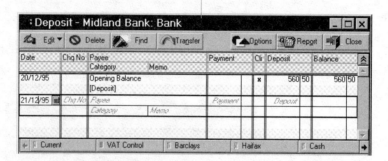

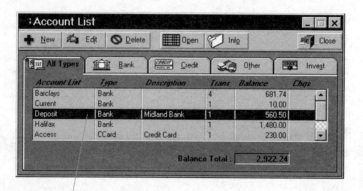

The account will also appear in the Account list.

Deleting an Account

Use this option with care, you will not be able to retrieve an account once it has been deleted.

Deleting anything in an accounts system should be done with caution. If the item deleted is used by other accounts it may well upset the whole balance of the system. This applies particularly to accounts, categories and classes.

1 From the main iconbar, click on the Accounts icon, or from the Lists menu, click on the Accounts option.

If you delete an account which already has transactions assigned to it, those transactions will also be deleted and there is no way of recovering them.

2 Click on the account to be deleted.

3 Click the Delete button.

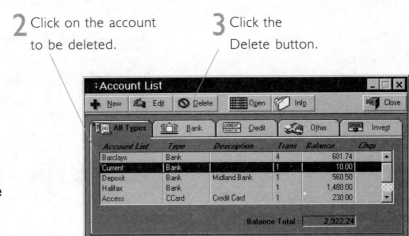

5 Click OK.

4 Confirm the request by typing 'YES'.

Click here to abort the procedure.

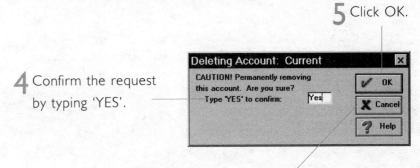

Adding a Category

Quicken is supplied with a large range of pre-defined categories to cover just about any situation. For ease of use, delete those that are not likely to be used. You can at a later stage add a new category or reinstate one that has been deleted.

1 From the Lists menu, click on the Categories & Transfer option to display the list of existing categories.

HANDY TIP

To quickly access the Set Up Category window press Ctrl+N.

2 Click on the New button.

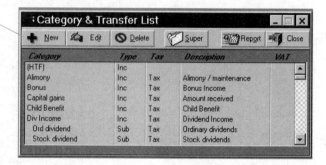

3 Enter the category name.

7 Click OK to finish.

4 Enter the category description.

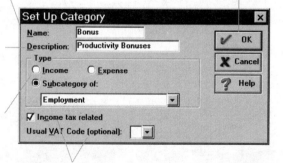

5 Click on the relevant type option. If it is to be a subcategory, select the category it is to be a subcategory of.

6 Click the Income Tax related option if you are going to use this category to track information required for your tax returns. If you are VAT registered you will have to specify the VAT code for this category.

Splitting a Category

There will be occasions when more than just one category or VAT rate apply to a single entry. Examples are when different types of Social Security payments are received by one cheque, or when items purchased at a supermarket are paid by one cheque.

1 In the account register, click on the category to be split and then click on the Splits button.

2 Enter the category or select from the drop-down list.

3 Enter VAT rate. Enter comments if required.

4 Enter the amount relevant for the category.

The VAT rate will only appear on your Splits window if you have chosen the VAT tracking option for that account.

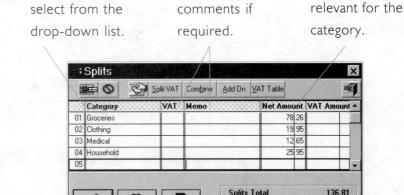

	Category	VAT	Memo	Net Amount	VAT Amount
01	Groceries			78	26
02	Clothing			19	95
03	Medical			12	65
04	Household			25	95
05					

Splits Total 136.81
Remainder 0.00
Transaction Total: 136.81

5 Continue until the cheque amount is allocated to the relevant categories. When complete click OK.

This window will appear different in the credit card account, where the options are Charge and Payment, and in the cash account where they are Spend and Receive.

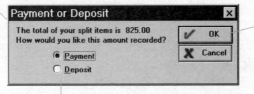

Payment or Deposit
The total of your split items is 825.00
How would you like this amount recorded?
● Payment
○ Deposit

7 Click the OK button, and then the Record button in the register window.

6 If no amount was entered in the register, before you entered the Splits option, you will be asked if the amount should be recorded as a Payment or a Deposit.

Deleting a Category

You should only delete a category after careful consideration.

You cannot delete a category that has subcategories, as these have to be deleted first.

When you delete a category, any transactions assigned to that category will also be deleted and will not be recoverable.

From the Lists menu, click on the Category & Transfer option.

2 Click on the category to be deleted.

3 Click on the Delete button.

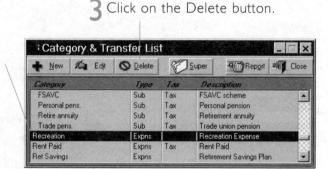

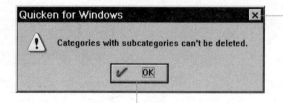

Click here to abort the deletion.

4 Click here to confirm the deletion.

Recategorising

It is often necessary to adjust or reorganise Quicken's categories during the course of a financial year. Without this feature, this task would be a time consuming chore.

As an example, you might want to incorporate bonus transactions with employment transactions, so doing away with the need for the bonus category.

Recategorising works in a similar way as Find and Replace, in that it searches for the text specified.

1 From the Activities menu, click on the Recategorise option.

2 Enter the category to be searched for or select one from the drop-down list.

3 Click here.

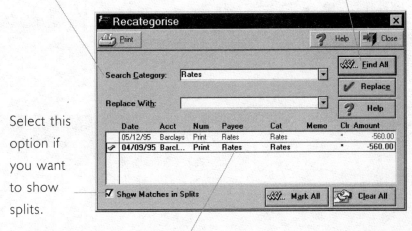

Select this option if you want to show splits.

HANDY TIP

Mark all or clear all transactions by clicking on the Mark All and Clear All buttons.

4 Click on the entries that have to be changed, so that they are marked with a tick.

5 Enter the name of the new category in the Replace With field.

6 Click the Replace button.

Adding a Class

Classes are used to provide an additional way of labelling your transactions. There are a number of ways they can be used, with most Quicken users treating them as subcategories. They do not replace categories but act as a second dimension to your reports, graphs and budgets.

As an example, you can use your personal current account for business and personal expenses, by leaving your personal transactions unclassified and assigning class names to your business transactions. When you come to produce reports, such transactions can be identified easily.

To quickly access the Class List press

Ctrl+L.

From the Lists menu, click on the Class option.

2 Click on the New button.

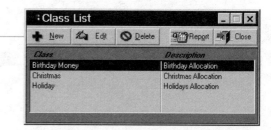

3 Enter the class name.

4 Enter the optional class description.

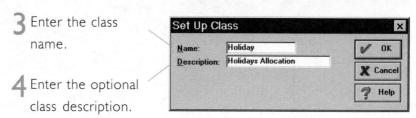

5 Click OK and the new class will appear in the Class List.

Using classes in the category field

To use a class in a transaction, first select the category, then type a slash '/' followed by the name of the class. If you want to use another class as a subclass, type a colon ':' followed by the name of the subclass.

Transferring between Accounts

From time to time it will become necessary to transfer funds between accounts.

A few such situations could be:

- When you pay money into a bank account from a cash account.
- When you pay off a credit card account from a bank account.
- When you withdraw from a cash dispenser - into your cash account.
- When you cash-in investments and pay the cheque into a bank account.
- Transferring money to, or from, a VAT account.

1 First display the account register you are transferring the money from, and click on the Transfer button.

2 Enter a description for the transfer. This may be carried forward from the register.

3 Enter the transfer date or click the right button to select from the calendar.

You can also transfer funds directly in both the Register and Write Cheques windows. Enter all the transaction information in the usual way, except for the Category field. Here type in the account name you want to transfer to and then click on the Record button.

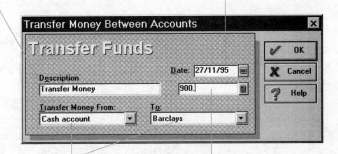

4 Select where the transfer is coming from and going to, from the drop-down lists.

5 Enter the transfer amount here (click the right button to display a calculator).

6 Click OK to finish. Quicken enters the name of the original account in the Category field, and creates the corresponding transaction in the other (target) account.

Quicken Colours

Quicken lets you define colours for each of its account types, so your current, deposit, cash and investment accounts can all have a distinctive set of colours, helping you to see which part of the program you are in.

To change the colours

1 From the main iconbar, click on the Register icon.

2 Click on the Options button.

3 Click on the Display tab, and then click on the Colours button.

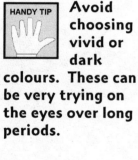

HANDY TIP

Avoid choosing vivid or dark colours. These can be very trying on the eyes over long periods.

4 Select a colour for each of your accounts from the pull-down list.

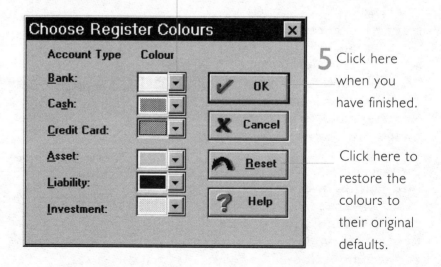

5 Click here when you have finished.

Click here to restore the colours to their original defaults.

CHAPTER THREE

Entering Transactions

The transactions you enter into your account can be from hand written cheques, deposits, cash dispenser transactions or from interest added to your account.

Quicken maintains a 'register' for each account. A register is where the history of transactions made on an account are recorded.

Whatever the transaction, it must be entered into the appropriate register. Quicken's transaction registers are set out in a similar way to your bank statements, so they are easy to follow.

Covers

Registers 36

Adding a Transaction 37

Configuring the Register 38

Paying Bills 40

Register Reports 41

Memorising Transactions 42

Deleting Transactions 44

Voiding Transactions 45

Finding a Transaction 46

Finding a Transfer 47

Find and Replace 48

Registers

The whole of the Quicken program revolves round the transaction entries you make. These are completed in registers, one for each account.

As with most manual bookkeeping systems, the entries are normally entered in two columns - the left for payments (debits) and the right column for receipts (credits). Other columns include date, description, cheque number, etc.. To make entering your accounts as simple as possible, Quicken has adopted the same principle.

To quickly re-enter the register you were working in last, click on the Register icon from the main iconbar.

Opening a register

1. Click on the Accounts icon from the main iconbar, to access the Account List window.

2. Double-click on the account you are going to make the entry in.

This will display the account's transaction register, containing your account details.

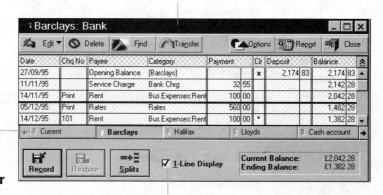

Click on the account button bar to quickly move from one account register to another.

The register will look slightly different if the 1-Line Display option is activated as the memo field will not be displayed.

Adding a Transaction

1 Enter the date either manually or click on the calendar button to the right of the field. Increase and decrease the date with the '+' and '-' keys.

2 Enter the cheque number, or alternatively, a reference number for other types of entries.

3 Enter the payee's name.

The 'Clr' column will remain blank at this stage. Later, when you have reconciled the entry with the bank statement, an 'X' will be displayed there.

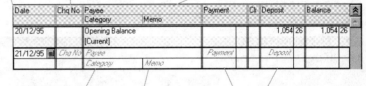

Date	Chq No	Payee		Payment	Clr	Deposit	Balance	
		Category	Memo					
20/12/95		Opening Balance				1,054 26	1,054 26	
		[Current]						
21/12/95	Chq No	Payee		Payment		Deposit		
		Category	Memo					

4 Enter the category the transaction is to be assigned to or select one from the drop-down list.

6 Enter in the Payment column the amount being paid out, or if it is money coming in then enter the amount in the Deposit column.

5 Enter an optional memo about the transaction here, if you have not opted for the 1-Line display.

To undo any mistake that may have been made during the entering or editing of a transaction, click on the Restore button.

7 Click the Record button. Quicken will now post the transaction so that the affected balances are updated. Then, it will make space for you to enter the next transaction.

Configuring the Register

From the Register Options window you can configure the way the register looks, sounds and behaves.

Click on the Register icon from the main iconbar and then click the Options button.

It is divided into three tabs - Display, Miscellaneous and QuickFill.

Click on the Display tab, to change the register's appearance.

The first three options define how the Register window is displayed.

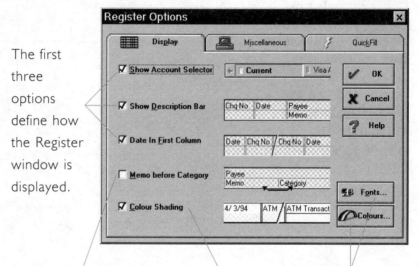

The next option swaps the memo and category columns around.

This adds shading to the transactions. It only adds shading to the lower line where a two line display is being used.

The Fonts and Colour options will allow you to define how your report will look.

...contd

3 Click on the Miscellaneous tab.

The Miscellaneous tab includes various warning options.

This option makes Quicken beep when you record or memorise a transaction.

When this option is selected, the Enter key moves between columns and then transactions.

Opens a single register window at any one time.

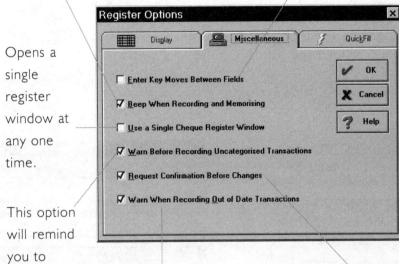

HANDY TIP

Categorising all of your transactions will make it easier to produce accurate reports, graphs and budgets.

This option will remind you to enter a category for each of your transactions.

Warns you if you try to record a transaction with a date from another year.

When this option is activated Quicken will ask you to confirm any changes when a transaction is completed.

4 Click on the QuickFill tab.

The QuickFill tab is where you specify what automatic entry features are to be used. These are already explained in Chapter 1.

Paying Bills

Bills can be paid in two ways - those we deal with directly and those that are paid for us automatically. The second category covers payments such as direct debits, and are detailed in the Chapter 4.

If you are completely up to date with your paperwork, you will be able to check the Quicken register(s) or reports to see your latest balance(s), and decide from which account the payment is to be made. Entering a payment into Quicken is almost identical to entering receipts.

1 Click on the account the payment is to be taken from.

2 Fill in the date, cheque number, payee, category and memo fields, and the amount in the Payment column.

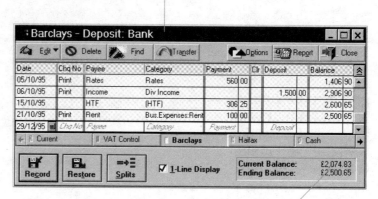

3 Once entered you will see the balance at the bottom of the window being reduced by the amount entered.

Register Reports

The Report button in the Register window lets you have a quick look at the transactions as they would be displayed in a report format. Quicken reports are covered in detail in Chapter 5.

HANDY TIP

To include all entries click on the new entry line in the register, otherwise the report will only show the transaction you are currently on.

1 Position the cursor on a new transaction entry line (at the bottom) in the register you are currently working in.

2 Click on the Report button.

Report

Click here to customise your report.

Click to print the report.

Click to finish.

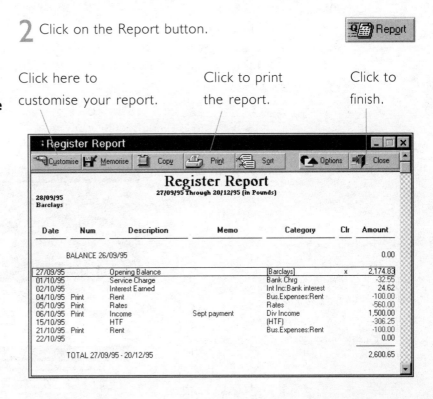

Memorising Transactions

Quicken allows you to save time by memorising frequently entered transactions. Typical examples of these would be standing orders or direct debits.

If configured correctly, Quicken can memorise each new transaction.

Memorising a new transaction manually

If the QuickFill option to automatically memorise new transactions is turned off, you can still instruct Quicken to memorise new transactions individually.

1 From the Lists menu, click on the Memorised Transaction option.

2 Click on the New button.

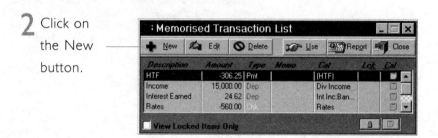

3 Select the type of payment.

4 Enter the details of the transaction as if you were entering the transaction in the register.

5 Click here when finished.

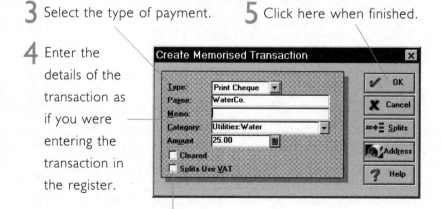

If you need to split the amount of the transaction between two or more categories, click on the Splits button.

Memorising transactions automatically

To use this facility, the QuickFill option "Automatic Memorisation of New Transactions" must be turned on.

1 Click on the Register icon from the main iconbar and then click on the Options button.

2 Select the QuickFill tab and then click on the "Automatic Memorising of New Transactions" checkbox.

A tick indicates that the option is switched on.

☑ **Automatic Memorisation of New Transactions**

Quicken will add new payees to the Memorised Transaction list as you record the transaction.

If you enter a transaction for a payee who is already on the Memorised Transaction list, the program updates the memo, amount and category, with this latest information. This will only be for new transactions. When you edit an existing transaction it will not be memorised automatically. You will have to memorise the edited transaction manually.

Deleting Transactions

It may be necessary to remove a transaction from your accounts.

Deleting a transaction wipes it off completely from the register. Cheque numbers will no longer be in sequence and if the transaction involved a transfer to another account, that link will also be deleted.

From the account register, click on the entry to be deleted.

2 Click on the Delete button.

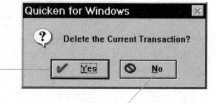

3 Click on the Yes button.

Click here to abort the procedure.

The transaction will now be permanently removed from the account register and the account balance will be automatically recalculated.

Voiding Transactions

Voiding a transaction leaves the entry listed in the register and enables you to continue maintaining your cheque number sequence, etc.. Quicken zeros the transaction amount and if the transaction involves a split, all amounts in the Split window will also be zeroed.

1 From the account register, click on the entry to be voided.

To quickly void a transaction, press Ctrl+V.

2 Click on the Edit menu.

Edit	
Undo	Alt+Backspace
Cut	Shift+Del
Copy	Ctrl+Ins
Paste	Shift+Ins
New Transaction	Ctrl+N
Edit	Ctrl+E
Delete Transaction	Ctrl+D
Insert Transaction	Ctrl+I
Void Transaction	**Ctrl+V**
Copy Transaction	
Paste Transaction	

3 Click on the Void Transaction option.

Quicken will void the transaction without asking for confirmation first.

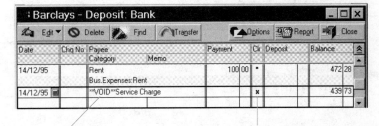

Date	Chq No	Payee / Category Memo	Payment	Clr	Deposit	Balance
14/12/95		Rent / Bus.Expenses:Rent	100 00	*		472 28
14/12/95		**VOID**Service Charge		x		439 73

The word 'VOID' is entered before the payee name.

An 'X' will also be displayed in the Clr column so that the entry does not conflict with reconciliation.

Finding a Transaction

You may need to find a transaction for a number of reasons, such as to edit it, to change its category, or even to void or delete the entry.

To find an entry

1 From the main iconbar, click on the Register icon.

2 Click on the Find button.

3 Enter some of the text you may remember from the transaction. This could be a category, name, amount or values in any other field, regardless of the case of the characters.

If you are searching for, say a category, it will be quicker to select the category option only, and not the All Fields option.

4 Define what part or parts of the transaction is to be searched.

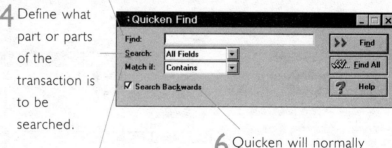

5 You can use a search criteria from the drop-down list.

6 Quicken will normally search from the first entry date through to the last.

If the transaction to be found is fairly recent, selecting the Search Backwards option may find the entry quicker.

7 Click on the Find button to find the first entry that matches your request. To search for other matching transactions click on it again. To list all of the matching entries found click on the Find All button.

If you double-click on an entry it will be displayed in its own transaction register.

Finding a Transfer

From time to time it may be necessary to look up the matching transfer entry in another transaction register.

To view a matching transfer

1 From the main iconbar, click on the Accounts icon.

2 Double-click on the account to open its register.

3 Click on the transaction that includes the transfer.

HANDY TIP

To select the Go To Transfer window quickly, press **Ctrl+X.**

4 Click on the Edit menu.

5 Click on the Go To Transfer option.

The register for the other account will be displayed with the cursor on the matching entry.

Find and Replace

HANDY TIP

The Find and Replace feature can also be used as just a find option.

You can use this feature to find a particular number or text and then replace it with an alternative. However, this option does not work with the Investment Register.

1 From the Edit menu, click on the Find and Replace option.

2 Enter the element you want to find.

3 Enter the search field and the search criteria from the drop-down lists.

4 Click the Find All button to display a list of matches here.

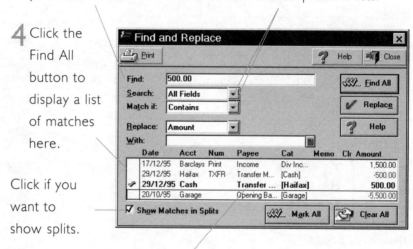

Find and Replace

Print | Help | Close

Find:	500.00			Find All
Search:	All Fields			Replace
Match if:	Contains			Help
Replace:	Amount			
With:				

Date	Acct	Num	Payee	Cat	Memo	Clr	Amount
17/12/95	Barclays	Print	Income	Div Inc...			1,500.00
29/12/95	Haifax	TXFR	Transfer M...	[Cash]			-500.00
29/12/95	Cash		Transfer ...	[Haifax]		✔	500.00
20/10/95	Garage		Opening Ba...	[Garage]			-5,500.00

☑ Show Matches in Splits | Mark All | Clear All

Click if you want to show splits.

HANDY TIP

Mark all or clear all transactions by clicking on the Mark All and Clear All buttons.

5 Click on the transactions to be replaced so that they are marked with a tick.

6 Select a field from the Replace drop-down list.

7 Enter the new details in the With field.

8 Click the Replace button.

CHAPTER FOUR

Financial Calendar

The new Financial Calendar feature is extremely useful, in that the calendar makes it easier for you to keep an eye on your future financial transactions, as well as displaying past transactions. So at a glance you can see transactions on a daily basis rather than viewing from several account registers.

You can use the calendar to display one-off transactions, for example payment of a cup final ticket, as well as recurring transactions, such as payment of your rent. Quicken lets you select the accounts and transactions you want displayed.

Covers

The Financial Calendar 50

Scheduled Transaction 52

Editing Scheduled Transactions 55

Deleting Scheduled Transactions 56

Paying Bills in Advance 57

Billminder 58

Reminders 59

Calendar Notes 60

The Financial Calendar

HANDY TIP

The **Financial Calendar window** can also be accessed by pressing Ctrl+J, or by clicking on the Activities menu and then clicking on the Financial Calendar option.

Opening the calendar

From the main iconbar, click on the Calendar icon.

Select whether to show register or schedule transactions, or show both.

Calendar   Memorised Transaction List

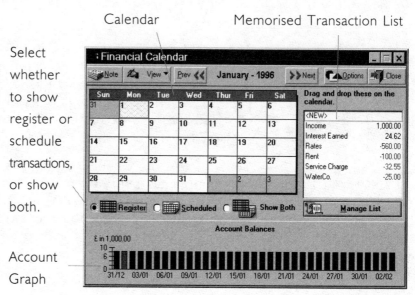

Account Graph

Viewing the calendar

There are several ways of displaying the calendar - the calendar together with the memorised transaction list and account graph, the calendar with the list or graph, or the calendar just by itself.

From the Calendar buttonbar, click on the view button.

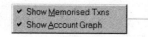

2 To deselect the options, click on them so that the ticks are removed.

Deselecting both options results in only the calendar being displayed in the Financial Calendar window.

Financial Calendar buttons

The two chevron arrows, when clicked, move the calendar backwards or forwards one month at a time.

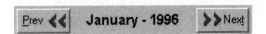

The Options button allows you to select the accounts to be included in the calendar and to alter the QuickFill options.

The two buttons at the bottom of the Accounts tab allow you to either mark all or clear all of the accounts in one go.

Click on an account to mark it for inclusion in the calendar. A second click will clear it.

Click on the QuickFill tab to define exactly how the facility is to operate.

The Manage List button gives you access to the Memorised Transaction list, which can then be amended.

Locking a memorised transaction means that you can enter other transactions for the same payee, but they must be for different amounts. If it is unlocked, the second entry overwrites the first.

Add   Edit   Delete

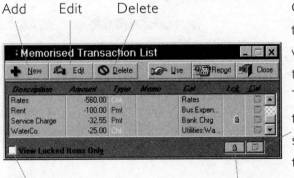

Click here, to view locked transactions.

Click on the transactions you want to appear in the calendar. Then, click on the Calendar icon so they appear in the calendar.

Click on the transaction to be locked and then click here.

Scheduled Transactions

Scheduled transactions are normally entries which are repeated each week, month, quarter or year. Typical examples are standing orders and direct debits with your bank.

Scheduling these transactions is the only way to be sure that such entries don't get overlooked - unless of course you can rely on your memory.

To list scheduled transactions

1 Click on the Lists menu.

2 Click on the Scheduled Transaction option.

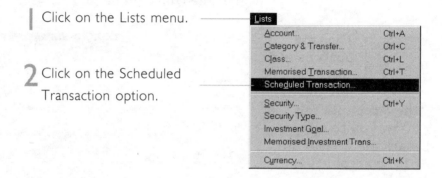

This window lists existing scheduled transactions, and offers the options of adding, editing and deleting entries.

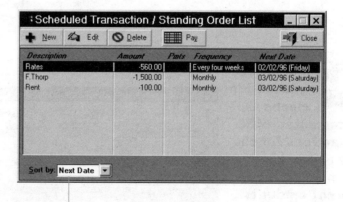

The scheduled transaction list can be sorted by next date, amount or description.

...contd

Adding scheduled transaction details

1 Click the New button, in the Scheduled Transaction window.

2 Enter the date for the next entry, and the account it is to be made from.

3 Select the scheduled transaction type - payment, deposit or print cheque.

4 Enter the payee name and an optional memo description.

Create Scheduled Transaction / Standing Order

Next Scheduled: 21/01/96
Account: Barclays

Type: Payment
Payee: AA
Memo: AA annual fee
Category: Motor
Amount: 62.25
Num Field: DirDeb

OK
Cancel
Splits
Address
Group
Help

Scheduled Transaction

Frequency: Yearly
Register entry: Automatically enter
Number of Payments: 999
Days in advance: 5

5 Select a category.

6 Enter the amount and type of payment.

7 Enter the transaction frequency.

8 Enter the number of payments and the number of days warning required.

HANDY TIP

Quicken defaults the number of payments to 999, so that you can record the transactions indefinitely.

Clicking on the Address button will allow you to enter the payee's address, but only if the scheduled transaction type is a Print Cheque.

Clicking on the Group button will allow you to access the Create Transaction Group window, where you can group a number of scheduled transactions together. If you regularly pay several bills at the same time, for instance at the beginning of the month, it will be a good idea to group them together.

Assigning a scheduled transaction to a payment date

HANDY TIP

To quickly select the Financial Calendar, press Ctrl+J.

1 From the Activities menu, click on the Financial Calendar option, or from the main iconbar, click on the Calendar icon.

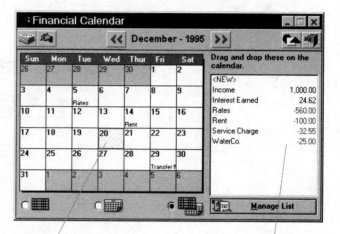

2 Move the mouse pointer over the entry from the Memorised Transactions panel, and hold down the left button on your mouse.

3 Drag the transaction to the date required in the Financial Calendar, and release the left button on your mouse.

Double-click on a date box if you want to read any text that is concealed in the box.

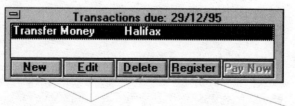

Click here to see the account register of the highlighted entry.

You can also add new entries or edit and delete entries.

Editing Scheduled Transactions

From time to time it may be necessary to change the details of a scheduled transaction, so it applies every time it takes place. Examples of this could be a change in a direct debit, insurance or loan rate amount. Changes in the payee's address could be another reason for editing at the schedule transaction level rather than at the individual entry level.

1 From the Lists menu, click the Scheduled Transaction option.

2 Click on the entry to be edited.

3 Click on the Edit button.

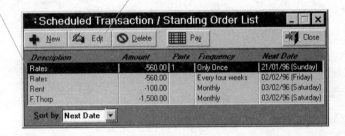

4 Change details as necessary. This window shows the same details as the Scheduled Transaction window.

 All changes will take effect from the next scheduled date.

5 Finally click here.

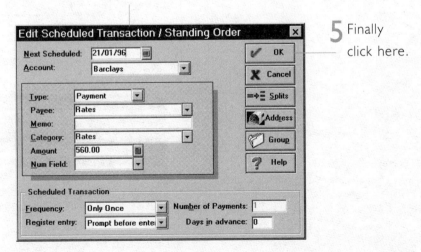

Deleting Scheduled Transactions

BEWARE

You cannot recover a deleted scheduled transaction. If you delete the wrong entry by mistake, you will have to enter it again.

You may have to do this if you have finished paying off the monthly instalments for (say) your car or monthly rent, which were paid by bank standing order. Now you need to delete the scheduled transaction that accounted for the payment.

1 From the Lists menu, click on the Schedule Transactions option.

2 Click on the entry to be deleted.

3 Click on the Delete button.

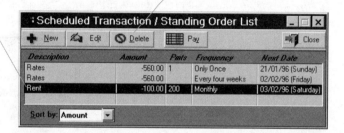

4 Click OK to confirm the deletion.

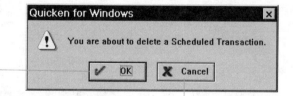

Click here to abort the procedure.

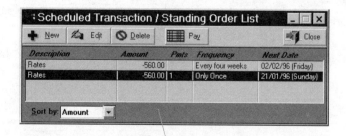

The transaction will be removed from the list.

Paying Bills in Advance

There may be occasions when you need to pay a scheduled transaction in advance of the scheduled date.

Typical examples could be where you need to clear the payment before the end of a financial year, or make the payment before closing down a bank account.

To pay a scheduled transaction in advance

1 From the List menu, click on the Scheduled Transaction option, to list all of the current scheduled transactions.

2 Click on the transaction to be paid.

3 Click on the Pay button.

This is similar to the Create Scheduled Transaction window.

4 Change the date as required.

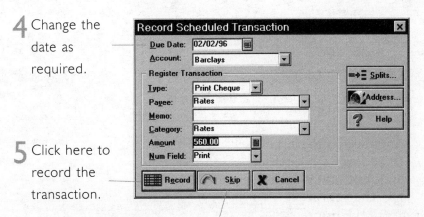

5 Click here to record the transaction.

The Skip button allows you to skip one payment, so that you continue paying from the following scheduled date.

The Splits button allows you to split the transaction into several categories, and the Address button lets you enter and store an address for printing on a cheque.

Billminder

Billminder is a feature that reminds you (either at DOS boot time or when you start Windows) of forthcoming bills that need to be paid, and of any action you need to take concerning your accounts.

When activated it will give you advance warning of bills to be paid with a window like this.

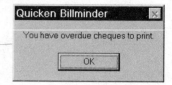

Changing Billminder's settings

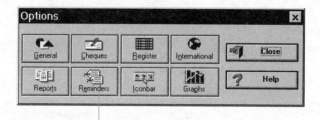

From the Edit menu, click on the Options button and then click on the Reminders option.

HANDY TIP

Your reminder interval can be anything from daily (1), to once a month (30), but make sure that the reminder interval is longer than the period between each Quicken session.

2 Click to clear the checkbox, and turn off Billminder. At the moment Billminder is activated.

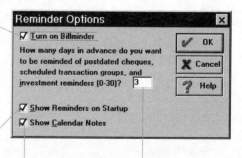

Click to clear this checkbox, if you prefer not to see the Reminder window each time you start the program.

3 Enter the number of days in advance you would like to be warned of forthcoming bills.

Click to clear this checkbox, if you don't want to see calendar notes in the Reminders window.

Reminders

To view the Reminders window when you are working in Quicken, click on the Reminders option, from the Activities menu.

Quicken's Reminders come in two forms: reminders of your own notes and reminders to pay accounts.

From the Activities menu, click on the Reminders option.

Click on the drop-down list to change the time period you want the notes shown from.

Click here to access the Reminder Options window (see the opposite page).

Panel, displaying notes from the selected time period.

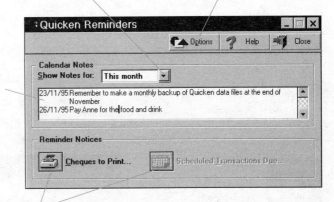

Click on these buttons to view lists of the cheques waiting to be printed and the due scheduled transactions.

Click on the account you want to open.

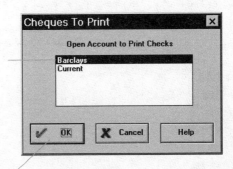

Click here to either print the cheques from the account selected or to enter the relevant scheduled transaction, depending on which Reminder Notices window you are in.

Calendar Notes

Sometimes it is handy to be able to jot down little notes about significant events.

Quicken provides the facility to attach notes to specific dates in the Financial Calendar.

1 From the Activities menu, click on the Financial Calendar option, from the main iconbar click on the Calendar icon.

2 Click on the month and date box.

3 Click the Note button.

4 Enter your comments or transaction schedule for that day.

5 Click the Save button.

Only one note at a time can be appointed to a date box.

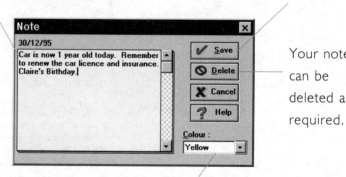

Your notes can be deleted as required.

You can use the different coloured notes to distinguish between business, financial and personal notes.

The colour of the notes background can be adjusted to suit your own preference.

When saved the note will appear as a little coloured square in the date box.

Click here, to view the note.

Cheques & Reports

You will save a lot of time and effort, as well as give your cheques a professional appearance, if you use Quicken to produce your cheques.

Quicken's reports make it easy for you to examine and interpret your account details. You can produce reports for either business or personal use. You can also customise them to suit your own requirements.

Covers

Writing Cheques 62

Cheque Options 63

Cheque Printer Setup 64

Printing Cheques 66

Reports 67

Customising Reports 68

Report Options 69

Reports Printer Setup 70

Printing Reports 71

Memorising Reports 72

Writing Cheques

Quicken gives you the option of writing cheques manually or offers the Write Cheques feature, to print your cheques from the system.

If you prefer to carry on writing your own cheques then enter the transaction details into the account register, making sure you enter Print in the Cheque Number field.

However, getting Quicken to prepare your cheques will save you a lot of time and trouble, especially if you're repeating a lot of the details. You will only have to enter the cheque details into Quicken once.

1 From the Activities menu, click on the Write Cheques option, or alternatively press Ctrl+W.

 When you've entered the cheque amount in figures, Quicken will automatically add it in words.

2 Enter the payee name.

3 Enter the date.

4 Enter the amount.

5 Enter the address.

 Enter the address if you are going to send your cheque out in a windowed envelope.

6 Type a memo, if required.

7 Select a category.

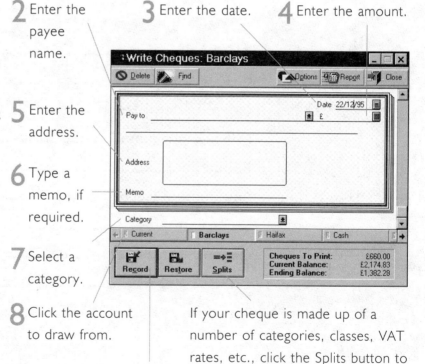

8 Click the account to draw from.

9 Click here to finish.

If your cheque is made up of a number of categories, classes, VAT rates, etc., click the Splits button to define the amounts individually.

Quicken will enter the transaction into the account register.

Cheque Options

Before you print cheques with Quicken, you are advised to set up the following options first. The options are found in the Cheques, Miscellaneous and QuickFill tabs.

I From the main iconbar, click on the Cheques icon and then click on the Options button.

2 Click on the Cheques tab.

Select the style of date you want printed on your cheques.

Activate the checkbox options you want to use by clicking on them so that a tick is displayed.

Cheque Options

| Cheques | Miscellaneous | QuickFill |

Printed Date Style
- ● MM/DD/YEAR
- ○ MM/DD/YY
- ○ DD/MM/YEAR
- ○ DD/MM/YY

✓ OK

✗ Cancel

? Help

☑ Print Categories on Voucher Cheques

☑ Warn if a Cheque Number is Re-used

☐ Change Date of Cheques to Date When Printed

☐ Artwork on Cheque Entry Screen   Sailboard ▾

Select to display artwork in the Write Cheques window. You can select the picture to be included from the drop-down list.

The artwork in the Write Cheques window will not get printed on the cheques but will just be displayed on screen.

Cheque Printer Setup

The Cheque Printer Setup lets you specify the printer you will be using, if you have more than one, and the cheque style.

I From the File menu, click on the Printer Setup option, and then click on Cheque Printer Setup.

2 Select the printer to be used.

3 Define paper type - single sheet, continuous or auto detect.

4 Click on one of these buttons to correctly position your cheque on the paper.

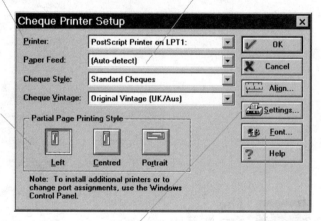

5 Click here if you need to alter your printer settings.

6 Click here to change your font settings.

Avoid using large or fancy fonts for your cheques. They are usually difficult to read.

7 Click on the font type, style and size you want to use on your cheques.

This panel displays how the currently selected font will look.

...contd

Aligning your cheques

1 Click on the Align button in the Cheque Printer Setup window.

Click here if inserting a full page of three cheques.

Click here if inserting two attached cheques.

Click here if inserting only a single cheque.

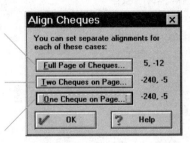

2 Clicking on your Align Cheque choice will take you into the Fine Alignment window.

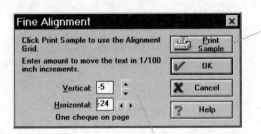

4 Click to print a sample cheque that includes a small alignment grid.

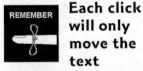
Each click will only move the text 1/100th of an inch.

3 Exactly position the printing of your cheque by clicking the up, down, left, right arrow buttons.

5 Click OK if you are happy with the alignment.

Printing Cheques

REMEMBER **Insert your cheques into the printer and make sure they are properly aligned. Turn your printer on and check to see that it is on-line.**

1 Open the account you want to print the cheques from.

2 From the File menu, click on the Print Cheques option.

Quicken will tell you how many cheques are ready to print.

3 Change the first cheque number if it does not tally with the first cheque in the printer.

HANDY TIP **If you want to print only some of the cheques, click on the Selected Cheques option. Then click on the Choose button. Click on and mark each cheque to be printed in the Select Cheques to Print window.**

4 Specify whether you are printing all cheques, cheques from a particular date or your own selected cheques.

5 Click on the Print button if you want to print the cheques all together or click Print First to print the first one, if you want to check the alignment.

6 In either case, the Print Cheques window will let you choose the style and type of cheques to be used, and the number to be printed on the page.

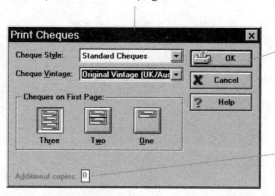

7 Click OK to print the cheques.

This option only applies if you are using voucher cheques.

Reports

There are a vast array of reports available to be used in Quicken and you can customise and memorise them as you like for use in the future.

HANDY TIP

Reports are available from most parts of the program and are accessed by clicking on the Reports button.

1 From the main iconbar, click the Reports icon.

2 Select the dates for the report.

4 Click the report type that most suits your requirements.

HANDY TIP

Don't include too much information on your reports. Cluttered reports are not easy to follow and may confuse.

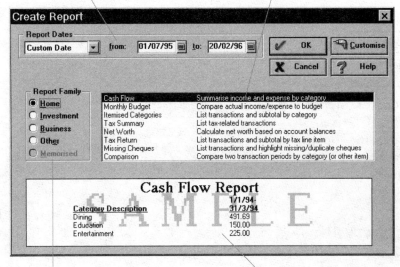

3 Click on the report family.

This panel displays a sample report of the type selected.

5 Click OK.

Report buttonbar.

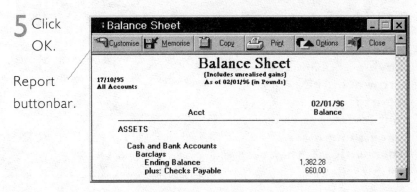

Customising Reports

Click on the Customise button in the Create Report window, or click on the Customise button on the Report buttonbar.

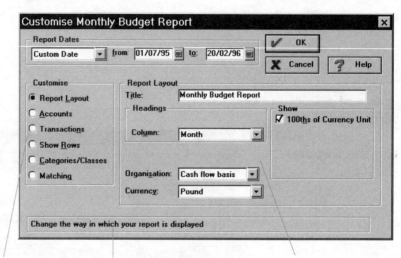

HANDY TIP If your report includes large figures, switch off the 100th of currency option to remove the pence units.

2 Click on the area to be customised.

3 Change the options in the Report Layout panel, these will vary depending on which area of the report is being customised.

HANDY TIP The QuickZoom feature lets you examine in detail each transaction which makes up the report. The QuickZoom Reports can be accessed by moving your mouse arrow over the report figures so that it changes to a magnifying glass filled with a Z, then double-click.

Panel informing you of what you can change in each section.

To change the title, dates and accounts label, position your mouse pointer over one of the labels so that it changes from an arrow to a magnifying glass, then double-click. The relevant part of Customise Report window will be displayed for you to edit.

Report Options

Before you start producing your reports, it may be necessary to configure Quicken to suit your own particular needs and those of your printer.

1 From the iconbar, click on the Options icon and then click on the Reports button.

2 Select how you want to see your accounts and categories displayed - as a name, description or both.

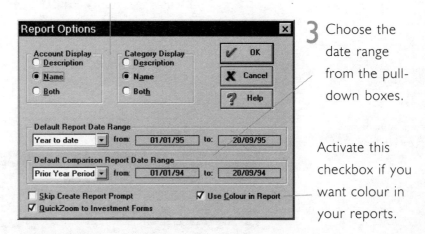

3 Choose the date range from the pull-down boxes.

Activate this checkbox if you want colour in your reports.

4 If you need to enter your own dates, select the Custom Date option and then fill in the dates boxes.

of a month, for example April 1, Quicken will take the last occurrence of the start date entered.

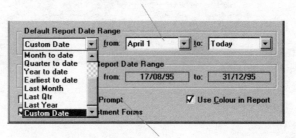

Activate the Skip Create Report Prompt checkbox if you don't want to see the Create a Report prompt each time you choose the Report option.

Report Printer Setup

From time to time, and at the end of your accounts year, you will probably need to print reports showing your financial situation. Good reports are a necessity if your accounts are to be passed to an accountant or for when you go cap-in-hand to your bank manager.

Before you even consider printing reports, you must make sure Quicken is correctly set up to print on your particular printer.

1 From the File menu, click Printer Setup.

2 Click on Report/Graph Printer Setup.

3 Select your printer.

Quicken's Auto-Detect option automatically detects the paper feed of your printer.

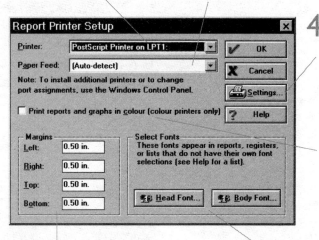

4 Click here to change the paper size and orientation.

Activate this checkbox to print reports in colour.

BEWARE

Avoid using large or fancy fonts on reports as they may be difficult to read, and may not be appreciated by your accountant.

5 Enter the page margins to indent the text.

6 Click here to change the fonts used in your report.

Printing Reports

1 Generate the report you want to print.

To quickly access the print window, press Ctrl+P.

2 From the Report buttonbar, click on the Print button, or from the File menu, click on the Print Report option.

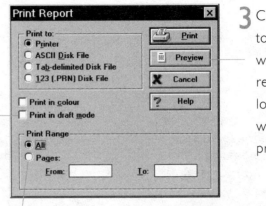

3 Click here to view what the report will look like when printed.

Draft mode allows faster printing, and should be selected for dot-matrix printers.

To print only a few pages, click on the Pages button and enter the page range in the From and To fields.

Check to see that the printer is switched on and has enough paper.

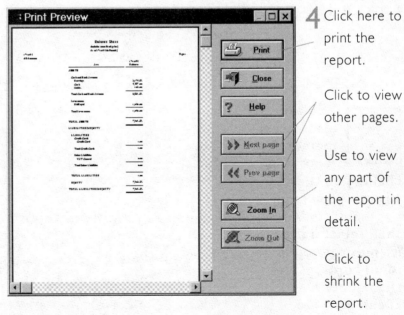

4 Click here to print the report.

Click to view other pages.

Use to view any part of the report in detail.

Click to shrink the report.

Memorising Reports

If you have taken the trouble to customise a report to suit your own needs, the last thing you want is to repeat the whole operation each time the report is required. Quicken provides a facility that can memorise your reports and display them in a list, for future selection.

1 Generate and customise the report (see earlier in this chapter).

2 From the Report buttonbar, click on the Memorise button.

If you enter an existing memorised report name, you may overwrite the existing report. However, Quicken will alert you to this before it happens.

3 Amend the report name, if required.

4 Click on the report date option you want to be included in the report.

5 Click here to memorise the report.

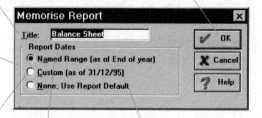

This option fixes the dates that were used in the report, so the same dates will be used for future reports too.

This option produces reports using Quicken default dates, i.e. those that appear in the Create Report Window.

You can also access memorised reports by clicking on the Reports icon from the main iconbar, then selecting the Memorised report family option, and then double-clicking on the report from the list.

This option lets Quicken recalculate the date each time the report is used, so that if you had requested a 'Month to date' report, the month will alter depending on the current date, and will start from the first day of the month.

Accessing a memorised report

1 From the Reports menu, click the Choose Memorised option.

2 Click on the report from the list, then click on the Use button. Finally click on the OK button, in the Create Report window.

CHAPTER SIX

Using Graphs

Use Quicken's graphs to spot trends in your spending and income patterns, to see how your net worth is changing and also to analyse your investment portfolio.

A graph will provide an instant indication of your finances, where as a text-based display or report may be more informative but will need detailed examination.

Covers

Creating Graphs 74

Graph Options 75

Budget Graphs 76

QuickZoom Graphs 77

Investment Graphs 78

Income and Expense Graphs 80

Net Worth Graphs 81

Customising Graphs 82

Printing Graphs 83

Memorising Graphs 84

Snapshots 85

Customising the Snapshots Page 86

Customising Individual Snapshots 87

Adding New Snapshot Pages 88

Creating Graphs

1 Click the Graphs icon from the iconbar.

2 Enter the start and end dates for the period you want your graph to cover.

3 Click on the type of graph you want to create.

4 Click the checkbox to include subcategories in your graphs.

When you produce graphs from accounts in different currencies, all amounts are converted to the 'home' currency (using the current exchange rate held in Quicken, see Chapter 12).

5 To show the graph in a different currency, select it from the currency drop-down list.

Create Graph

From: 1/95   To: 10/95

Graph To Create
- ● Income and Expense Graph
- ○ Budget Variance Graph
- ○ Net Worth Graph
- ○ Investment Graph

☐ Show subcategories in graph

Currency: Pound

Income and Expense Filters

✓ Accounts...   Categories...   Classes...

✓ Create
✗ Cancel
Memorised...
? Help

6 Click here, to select the accounts to be included in the graph.

7 Click here, to select only certain categories.

8 Click here, to select only certain classes.

Once in the Filters window, you can include and exclude items by clicking on them. A tick next to an item indicates that it will be included in the graph. When finished, click OK.

Once a filter has had items excluded a tick will appear next to the filter name in the Create Graph window.

9 Finally, click on the Create button, to generate your graph.

Graph Options

Selecting the Display Patterns on Screen option, may print graphs in black and white even on a colour printer.

This group of options control how the program displays graphs on your monitor, and how they are printed.

1 In the Graph window, click on the Options button, or from the main iconbar, click on the Options icon and then on the Graphs button.

2 Click on this checkbox to produce black and white patterns instead of solid colour graphs which can speed up printing.

3 Click here to view graphs in their own separate windows, instead of two in each window.

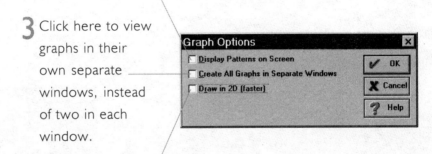

The Draw in 2D option may be more suitable for slower computers.

4 Click on this checkbox to get the graph displayed faster. The default is 3D, which is more attractive, but takes longer to produce.

Budget Graphs

For comparing your actual and budget figures, a graph is more effective in spotting the differences than a table with a set of figures.

Budgetary variance graphs compare your 'actual' spending and income with 'budgeted' spending and income. Quicken calculates the difference between the two, so that you can see how you are actually doing, compared to the budget.

Naturally, before you can create this type of graph, you must set up a budget, and this is explained in Chapter 8.

1 From the Reports menu, click on the Graphs option and then click on the Budget Variance option.

2 Enter the graph dates.

3 Select this checkbox to include subcatergories.

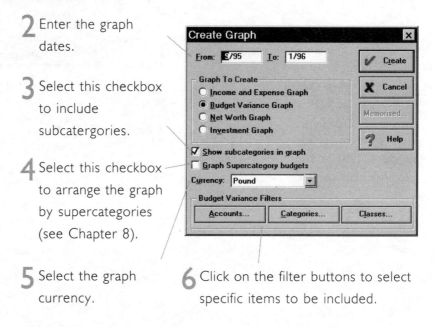

4 Select this checkbox to arrange the graph by supercategories (see Chapter 8).

5 Select the graph currency.

6 Click on the filter buttons to select specific items to be included.

7 Click the Create button to view your graph.

QuickZoom Graphs

By double-clicking with the mouse when the cursor icon changes to a QuickZoom magnifying glass, you can get Quicken to display a detailed in-depth Graph covering that particular element.

Move your mouse arrow over an element, so that it changes to the QuickZoom magnifying glass and then double-click.

To view the exact amount of an element, move your mouse pointer over it (so that it changes to the QuickZoom magnifying glass), then hold down your right mouse button.

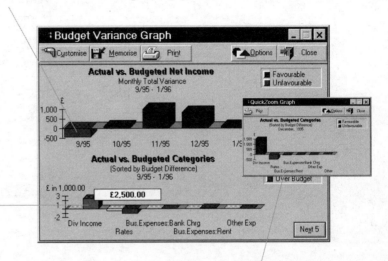

You will now see the QuickZoom graph.

If you repeat the procedure on one of the elements in the QuickZoom graph window, you will QuickZoom to a report.

To get back to the previous graph press the Escape key on your keyboard.

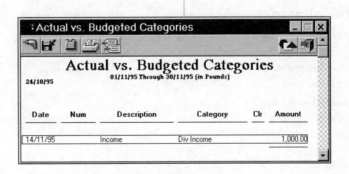

Investment Graphs

Investment graphs are invaluable in spotting trends in shares and in your investment portfolio.

1 From the Reports menu, click on the Graphs option and then click on the Investments option.

2 Enter the graph period dates.

3 Select the graph currency.

4 Click the filter buttons, to select the items to be included.

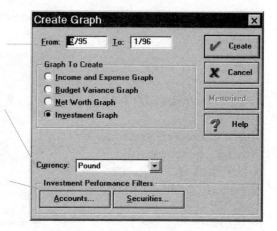

5 Click on the Create button, to view your graph.

By double-clicking on the elements, you can produce additional graphs, further detailing the information shown. Double-clicking in the QuickZoom graph will bring up a report.

The upper graph shows how the value of your investment portfolio has changed over the period selected.

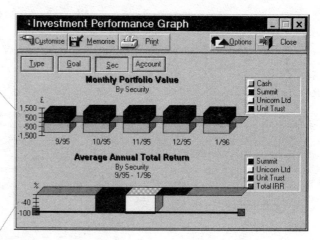

The lower graph shows how well each part of your portfolio has performed, compared to the portfolio as a whole.

...contd

Changing how the graph is summarised

In the Investment Performance Graph window, there are four option buttons. These options provide you with various ways of viewing the data used in the graph.

The default option is set so that the graph is summarised by security, but you can also summarise it by account, security type or goal.

> Click on the option type you want the graphs summarised by, in this case by account.

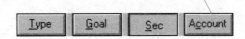

The graph will change to show the monthly portfolio value and average annual total return by account.

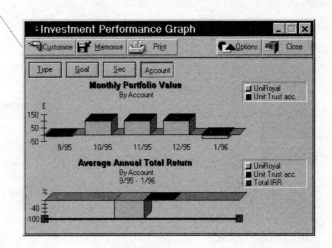

Income and Expense Graphs

To produce a graph which shows you what your spending patterns are:

1 From the Reports menu, click on the Graphs option and then the Income and Expense option.

2 Enter the dates for the period the graph is to cover.

3 Click this checkbox, to include subcategories.

4 Select the graph currency.

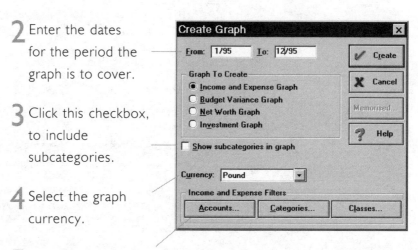

5 Click the filter buttons to select the items to be included.

6 Click the Create button to view your graph.

By double-clicking on the elements, you can produce additional graphs, further detailing the information shown. Double-clicking in the QuickZoom graph will bring up a report.

The bar chart displays income and expenses over the time period you selected.

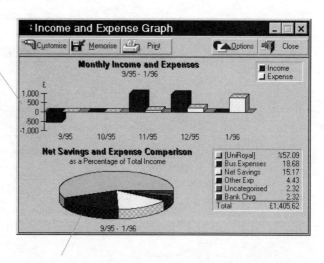

The pie chart displays what has happened to your income.

Net Worth Graphs

The major difference between the Net Worth Graphs and the Income and Expense Graphs is that the latter uses figures from categories. Net Worth Graphs use figures from the actual accounts, such as bank accounts and credit cards.

1 From the Reports menu, click on the Graphs option and then click on the Net Worth option.

2 Enter the graph period dates.

3 Select the graph currency.

4 Click on the filter buttons to select specific items to be included.

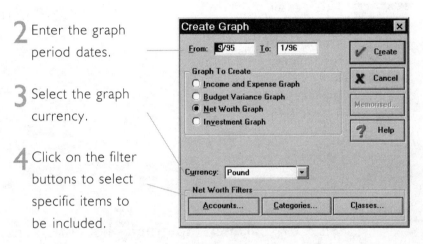

5 Click on the Create button, to view your graph.

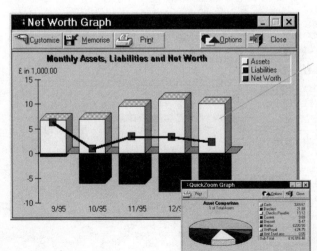

To access the QuickZoom graph, move your mouse pointer over an element and double-click.

REMEMBER

Double-clicking on an element in the QuickZoom graph will produce a report showing the actual figures.

Customising Graphs

Quicken gives you considerable flexibility in creating graphs to suit your own requirements. It is possible to define graphs' date range and currency, in addition to accounts, categories and classes shown in it.

From the Graph window, click on the Customise button window.

This graph can be memorised for future use (see the Memorising Graphs section on page 84).

Make the changes you want to the date range, currency and filters. These changes will not be saved unless you memorise the graph.

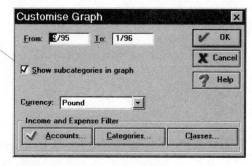

Click on the OK button, to display the customised graph.

Removing graph elements

You can remove individual elements from bar graphs and pie charts.

Once an element has been removed it can only be recovered by creating the graph again.

Hold down the Shift key and click on the element with the left mouse button.

The element has now been removed.

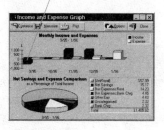

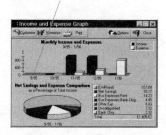

Printing Graphs

REMEMBER

Before you print your graph, make sure Quicken is configured to work correctly with your printer.

From the File menu, click on the Printer Setup option, and then click on Report/Graph Printer Setup.

2 Select your printer.

Quicken's Auto-Detect option automatically detects the paper feed of your printer.

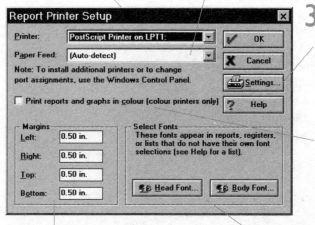

3 Click here to change the paper size and orientation.

Activate this checkbox to print reports in colour.

HANDY TIP

When selecting fonts for graphs, avoid large, fancy or bold type faces.

4 Enter the page margins to indent the text.

5 Click here to change the fonts in your graphs.

Memorising Graphs

Having spent some time creating a graph that meets your requirements, the last thing you will want to do is to have to recreate it time and time again.

Quicken gives you the opportunity to save your graph, so that it can be reproduced at a later stage.

1 Create the graph to be memorised.

2 Click on the Memorise button.

HANDY TIP

If you enter a name which already exists as a memorised graph, Quicken will alert you.

3 Enter a suitable name.

4 Click OK, to memorise the graph.

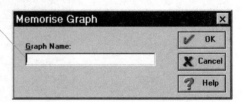

Accessing a memorised graph

1 From the Reports menu, click on the Memorised Graphs option.

2 Double-click on the graph to be recalled, or click on the graph title and then on the Use button.

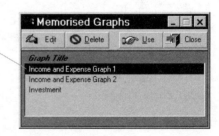

REMEMBER

If you make any changes to your graph, and if you want to save the changes, you will have to 'memorise' it again.

3 Enter the date range and then click on OK, to produce the graph.

Snapshots

Quicken's Snapshots feature allows you to view all your finances on one screen. You can view up to 6 small Snapshots on the screen at a time.

Viewing Snapshots

From the Reports menu, click on the Snapshots option.

Unless you have configured it otherwise, the window displayed will show 6 panels, each with a graph, text, slide bar or notes.

If you position your mouse cursor over one of the Snapshots section and hold down the left mouse button, then the amount representing that element will be shown.

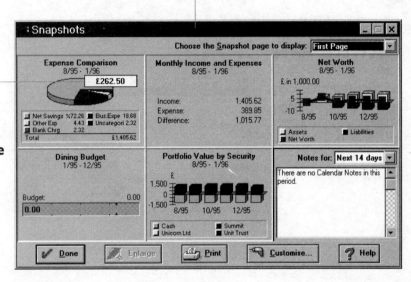

You can also access the expanded graphs by clicking on any panel and then clicking the Enlarge button.

Expanding graphs using the QuickZoom feature

As you move your mouse cursor over certain elements in the window, you will see the cursor arrow changing into the QuickZoom magnifying glass icon.

When the QuickZoom icon appears over the Snapshot window, double-click. The expanded graph of that Snapshot will now be displayed.

Customising the Snapshots Page

Click the Customise button in the Snapshots page.

2 Select how many Snapshots are to be displayed in the Snapshots page (window).

3 Click on the panel you want to customise.

 REMEMBER **Calendar notes, savings goals and budgets must all be created before you can display them in the Snapshots page.**

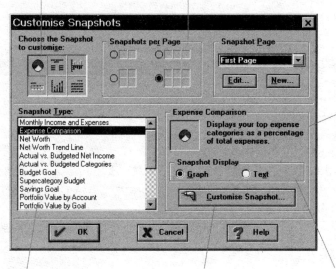

This panel gives a brief description of the details displayed.

4 Click on the Snapshot type you want displayed.

Click on here to further customise your chosen Snapshot (see opposite page).

5 Select if the panel is to show a graph or text.

Customising Individual Snapshots

The Customise Snapshot page displayed will vary according to the Snapshot selected.

1 From the Customise Snapshots window, click on the Customise button.

2 Select the date range from the drop-down list.

3 Activate this checkbox to include subcategories.

4 Select the Snapshot currency.

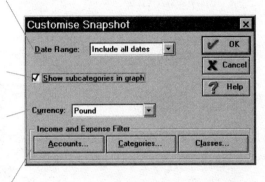

5 Click the filter buttons to select specific items to be included.

6 Click on the items you want to include in the Snapshot, so that they are marked with a tick.

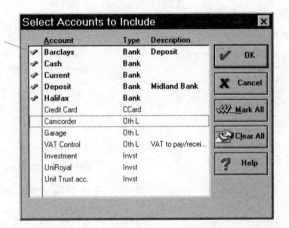

7 Click OK, to finish in this window and then OK again to finish customising the Snapshot.

Adding New Snapshot Pages

REMEMBER

You can also add a new Snapshot by clicking on the New button in the Edit Snapshot Pages window.

1 From the Customise Snapshots window, click on the New button.

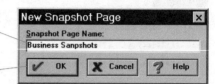

2 Enter a name.

3 Click on the OK button.

4 Select the number of Snapshots you want in the new window.

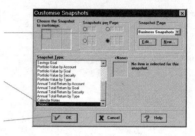

5 Click on the Snapshot types.

6 Click OK.

Editing and deleting Snapshot pages

1 From the Customise Snapshots window, click on the Edit button.

2 Click on the Snapshot page to be edited or deleted.

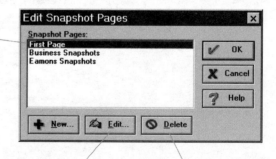

Click on the Edit button to change the name of the Snapshot page.

Click on the Delete button to delete the Snapshot page.

CHAPTER SEVEN

Reconciling Accounts

It is important to keep your Quicken records balanced with your bank and building society records. When you receive your statement, match entries on it to those in the account register and make sure that you are aware of the uncleared items. This exercise should be done on a fairly regular basis.

Covers

Balancing Accounts 90

Reconciling Accounts 91

Reconciling a Bank Statement 92

Reconciling Unit Trust Accounts 95

Reconciling Investment Accounts 96

Reconciling a Credit Card Statement 98

Updating Cash/Share Balances 100

Balancing Accounts

Entering transactions into Quicken for the whole of a financial year is next to pointless, if at the end of that period the books don't balance.

Many people seem to think that keeping a record of all transactions is all that is required of bookkeeping. Unfortunately, that is only part of it. One of the essential requirements is to ensure that your computerised bookkeeping system reflects the actual events occuring in your financial life.

 At the end of the financial year, all the monies you received must match exactly the monies you spent plus any you have in your account.

For each account you have in Quicken, you should be able to balance it with the actual records on paper, such as statements from the bank or invoices from a company.

Balancing accounts means that the figure at the end of the statement (the amount you had in your account on the date of the statement), should match with that held in Quicken, taking into account things like cheques which may still have to be presented.

If the balance doesn't match, don't continue entering new transactions until the problem is resolved. If you leave it too late, it will inevitably take much longer to work out.

Reconciling Accounts

For Quicken to work for your benefit and for it to provide you with the correct results, you'll need to do a bit more than just enter transactions.

Failure to check your transactions on a regular basis can mean that your accounts may not balance at the end of the financial period, and that a lot of time and effort will have to be spent to put the problem right.

Entering the details of a cheque or credit card payment to a supplier will be next to useless if the recipient either does not agree with the amount or makes a mistake over it, or if you make an error entering the figure.

All of these things could mean that your accounts do not balance, with statements you receive from organisations you bank or deal with.

It is essential that you check all your transactions against the various invoices, statements and receipts you receive.

Reconciling is a relatively straightforward business. Most bank or building society statements show two columns in the same way as in Quicken's registers. The left column is usually for payments and the right for receipts. The names at the top of the column may differ, but basically they have the same function.

Reconciling a Bank Statement

1 Open the account register to be reconciled.

2 From the Activities menu, click on the Reconcile option, or from the main iconbar, click on the Reconcile icon.

3 Enter the opening balance and ending balance, from your bank statement.

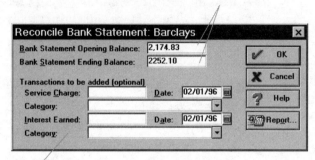

4 Enter any service charges or interest earned details.

5 Click on the OK button.

The window displayed shows all appropriate entries.

 HANDY TIP

If you have a large group of transactions to mark as cleared, click on the first transaction and hold down the left mouse button, next move the mouse pointer down the list and then release the mouse button.

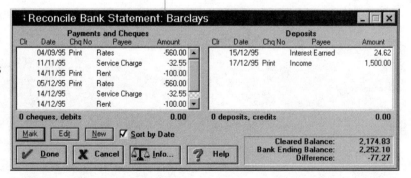

6 Click on each entry in the list that also appears on the statement, so that it is marked with a tick.

✔ 04/09/95 Print	Rates		-560.00
✔ 11/11/95	Service Charge		-32.55
✔ 14/11/95 Print	Rent		-100.00
✔ 05/12/95 Print	Rates		-560.00
✔ 14/12/95	Service Charge		-32.55
✔ 14/12/95	Rent		-100.00
✔ 22/12/95 Print	A.A.		-62.25

You will not only be able to match the entries with those on the bank statement, but will also have indirectly marked the transaction in the register as being cleared.

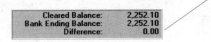

Date	Chq No	Payee	Category	Payment		Clr	Deposit		Balance	
14/11/95	Print	Rent	Bus.Expenses:Rent	100	00	x			1,420	03
05/12/95	Print	Rates	Rates	560	00	x			860	03

At the end of this process, the difference displayed in the lower right corner of the window should be £0.00 (zero).

Cleared Balance:	2,252.10
Bank Ending Balance:	2,252.10
Difference:	0.00

7 Click on to the Done button when the transactions have been marked.

This window will be displayed if your account has balanced.

When your account does not balance

When your account does not reconcile properly, you can use the Edit and New buttons, in the Reconcile Bank Statement window, to adjust and add to the transactions in the register. Typical examples of this is where the bank has made an unexpected charge, or a direct debit amount has changed.

If you click on the Done button while there is still a balance outstanding, Quicken will give you the opportunity to automatically adjust the balance.

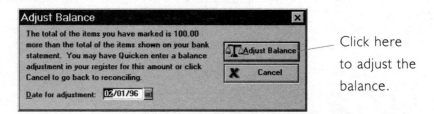

Click here to adjust the balance.

REMEMBER **While adjusting the balance in this way may seem like a quick and easy way out of the problem, the new entry in the register still has to be completed with a payee name and category, etc.. Also a document for the transaction will be needed.**

Click here only if you want to create a report.

Click here to complete the reconciliation.

This will produce an entry in the register for the amount of the imbalance.

Date	Chq No	Payee	Category	Payment		Clr	Deposit		Balance	
15/12/95		Interest Earned	Int Inc:Bank interes			x	24	62	752	10
17/12/95	Print	Income	Div Income			x	1,500	00	2,252	10
22/12/95	Print	A.A.	Other Exp	62	25	x			2,189	85
02/01/96		Balance Adjustment		100	00	x			2,089	85
04/09/95		Chq No	Payee	Category	Payment			Deposit		

Reconciling Unit Trust Accounts

With the statement received for your unit (investment) trust account, you can clear each entry shown and adjust the share balance as necessary. Quicken will automatically update the market value if you type in the ending price per share.

1 Open the account to be reconciled.

2 From the Activities menu click on the Reconcile option, or from the main iconbar click on the Reconcile icon.

3 From the details listed on the statement, enter in the starting and ending share balances.

4 Enter the ending price per share.

> Reconcile Share Balance Account: Inv... ☒
> Starting share balance: 200
> Ending share balance: 250
> Ending price per share: 3.00
> (optional)
> Statement ending date: 02/01/96
> ✓ OK
> ✗ Cancel
> ? Help

5 If necessary, you can change the statement ending date to match that of the statement.

6 Click here to continue.

7 For each entry shown on the statement, click on the corresponding transaction in the list, so that a tick is displayed in the Clr column.

8 Click here and the account is reconciled.

When completed the difference here should be £0.00 (*zero*).

Reconciling Investment Accounts

On receiving a statement from your broker, you can clear each transaction appearing on your statement and adjust the transaction register as necessary. When complete, you can go to the Quicken Portfolio View window to update your security prices.

1 Open the account to be reconciled.

2 From the Activities menu, click on the Reconcile option, or from the iconbar click on the Reconcile icon.

3 Enter the starting and ending balance, from your account statement.

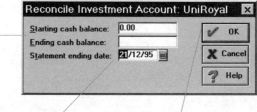

4 Where necessary, change the statement ending date to reflect the statements.

5 Click here to continue.

6 Click on the transactions that appear on the statement. A tick will be added in the Clr column.

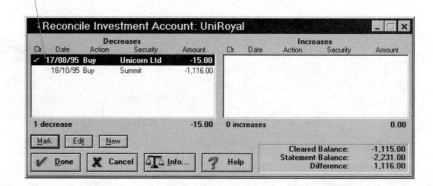

...contd

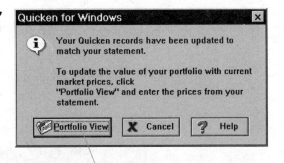

7 Click on the Done button.

If your account is not reconciled, you can let Quicken make the adjustments for you, but remember to complete the adjustment transactions in the register.

At the end of this process, the difference will be displayed in the lower right corner of the window and should be £0.00 (zero).

8 Finally, click here to enter the Portfolio View window.

Quicken gives you the chance to enter the latest share prices from your statement into your portfolio (for more details on using the Portfolio View window see chapter 10).

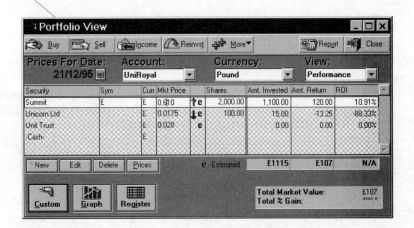

Reconciling a Credit Card Statement

Normally reconciling a credit card account involves checking the statement and paying the bill.

1 Open the account to be reconciled.

2 Click on the Activities menu and then click on the Pay Credit Card Bill option.

3 Compare the previous balance in the window with your previous statement's balance. If the amounts differ, overwrite the window balance with the statement balance.

REMEMBER

The balance shown in the Previous Balance box and your statement should be the same, as they should have matched at the end of the last statement.

4 Enter the new statement balance.

Credit Card Statement Information: Credit Card

Previous Balance: -1245.62
New Balance:

Transaction to be added (optional)
Finance Charges: 62.5   Date: 19/12/95
Category: Bus.Expenses:Bank Chrg

OK
Cancel
Help

5 If there are interest charges or fees, type in the appropriate amount, date and category.

6 Click here to continue.

7 For all entries on your statement, click on the corresponding transaction in the list, so that a tick is displayed in the Clr column.

8 Click here and the account will be reconciled.

Pay Credit Card Bill: Credit Card

Charges / Payments

19/12/95 Finance Charges   62.50   18/10/95   -1.00

0 charges, debits   0.00   0 payments, credits   0.00

Mark Edit New   Cleared Balance: -61.50
Done Cancel Info Help Statement Balance: 1.00
                          Difference: -62.50

When completed the difference here should be £0.00 (*zero*).

Making a credit card payment

When the difference in the Pay Credit Card window is zero you can make the credit card payment.

You have the choice of either writing a hand written cheque, which can be recorded in the account register, or getting Quicken to print one for you. In this example, we will be printing the cheque.

1 Open the credit card account and then reconcile it.

2 Select the account to pay from.

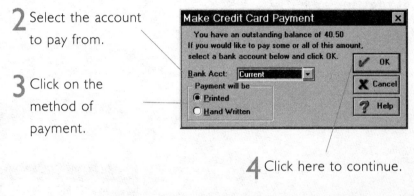

REMEMBER **The Hand Written option will take you into the Register window, and the Printed option will take you to the Write Cheques window.**

3 Click on the method of payment.

4 Click here to continue.

5 Fill in the cheque details.

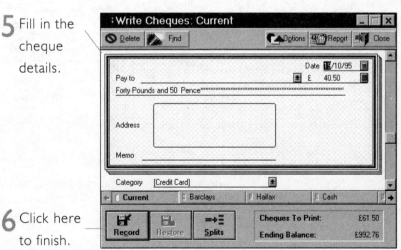

6 Click here to finish.

Updating Cash/Share Balances

There are times when trying to match your figures in the system with the balance in the manual records just seems impossible, but whatever happens, at the end of your financial year, the figures have to balance.

Quicken has included a little feature to help you with this, however it should only be used as a last resort.

Only cash accounts and share accounts can use this option because bank, credit card and investment accounts should be matched with their statements.

When possible, enter transactions on a daily basis so that there is less chance of forgetting an entry.

1 Before you can use this feature, you must first open either a cash or shares register.

2 From the Activities menu, click the Update Balances option.

3 Select either the Update Cash Balance or Update Share Balance option. This is dependant on which register is open.

4 Enter the new account balance.

Update Account Balance

Update this account's balance to: `132.5`

Category for adjustment: `Gift Received`
(optional)

Adjustment date: `19/01/96`

✔ OK

✗ Cancel

? Help

5 Select a category for the imbalance, from the drop-down list.

6 Enter the adjustment date.

7 Click on the OK button. The transaction will be entered into the register and marked as a balance adjustment.

CHAPTER EIGHT

Budgeting & Loans

Quicken allows you to set financial goals by any category, and then it enables you to compare your targetted incomings and outgoings with actual figures.

This chapter explains how this is done. It also includes a section on savings goals, which is a way of making funds unavailable or "hiding" them, from one of your accounts, so that it can be put aside for something you want.

Quicken can also help you to plan, pay for and then keep track of your loans. This is also covered in this chapter.

Covers

Budgets and Targets 102

The Budget Window 103

Manually Entering Budget Figures 104

Entering Existing Budget Figures 105

Tidying up the Budget Window 106

Moving Around the Budget Window 108

Using the Progress Bar 109

Savings Goals 110

Setting up a Loan 112

The View Loans Window 113

Entering Loan Details 114

Paying Loans 116

Budgets and Targets

With budgets or targets, the aim is to achieve the goals set. This may be target figures you enter yourself, or simply based on the previous year's figures.

Budgeting, therefore, consists of two sets of figures. The target you have set (or last year's figures), and the current figures.

Obviously, the best way to set budgets is to base them on past performance, but there are situations where this may not be possible, or may be unsuitable:

- If you have no figures for a previous financial year.

- When the figures of the previous year are lower or higher than average or where these figures are not suitable predictors.

Some businesses set a percentage increase, say of 10%, over the previous year's figures.

The Budget window

Quicken offers two ways of setting up your budgets, and both are done in the Budget window. The Budget window allows you to either enter your own figures into the entry screen or select a previous year's figures. Both options are detailed in this chapter.

| From the Plan menu, click on the Budgeting option.

The entry screen is made up of three sections; the category list, the column totals and the row totals.

The category list. Income categories appear above the expense categories.

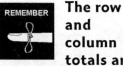

The row and column totals are derived so entries cannot be made directly into them.

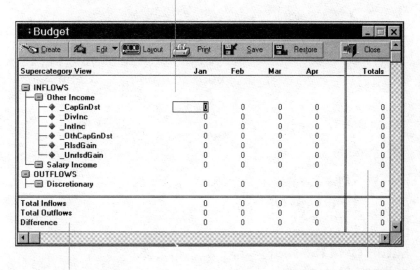

The column totals.   The row totals.

Manually Entering Budget Figures

You may decide to enter the figures manually or you may just need to edit the entered amounts. You can do both in the same way as you would in a spreadsheet.

| Click on the relevant cell and enter the amount.

If you make a mistake, the Esc key will restore the amount previously held in the cell.

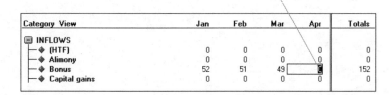

Category View	Jan	Feb	Mar	Apr	Totals
⊟ INFLOWS					
─◆ (HTF)	0	0	0	0	0
─◆ Alimony	0	0	0	0	0
─◆ Bonus	52	51	49		152
─◆ Capital gains	0	0	0	0	0

2 Click on the Save button when you have entered the figures.

Duplicating the same figures

This is a quick way of entering identical figures, in a row or column, in one go. It eliminates the need for you to enter the same figures in each cell separately.

| Enter a figure in the first cell.

To zeroise amounts in rows or columns, enter 'O' in the first cell and then click on the Edit button and then the Clear Row option.

2 Click on the Edit button.

3 Click on either Fill Rows Right or Fill Columns option.

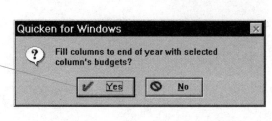

4 Click the Yes button. The figure will now be displayed in all the cells in that row or column.

Entering Existing Budget Figures

You can also use existing information in your account registers as the budget figures.

| From the Budget window, click the Create button.

 The new figures in the listing from your account will overwrite any data you may have entered previously into the Budget window. Click on the Restore button to bring them back.

2 Select the dates required.

3 Select how the amounts are to be shown.

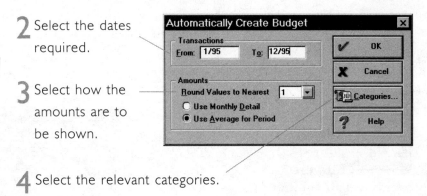

4 Select the relevant categories.

5 Click OK. The figures will be entered into the listing.

Exporting budget figures

If you use a spreadsheet you may like to 'export' the Budget figures to it.

| From the Budget window, click on the Edit button.

2 Click on the Copy All option.

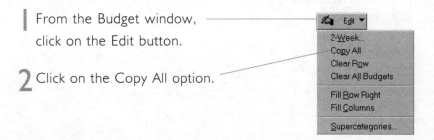

Your figures will be placed in the Windows Clipboard and can be pasted directly to popular spreadsheets such as Lotus 123 or Excel.

Tidying up the Budget window

The Budget window contains so much information that trying to view it all will involve a great deal of scrolling around.

Removing all default category lines with zero amounts in them will help to ease the situation. There are also considerable number of categories in Quicken and many of these may never be used, and so only get in the way.

In the Budget window, click on the Layout button.

You can tidy up your Budget window still further by hiding transfers and supercategories. This is done by clicking on the Show Transfers and Show Supercategories checkboxes (so that the ticks in them are removed).

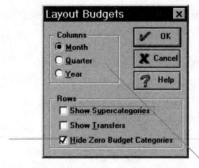

2 Click on this checkbox.

By clicking on the Quarterly or Yearly columns options as long as monthly budget figures are not essential, you can probably display all, or most of your figures, in one window.

...contd

Supercategories

Click on the Layout option in the Budget window and click on the Show Supercategories option to see your supercategories.

Supercategories are a way of grouping together related categories and subcategories into higher level groups, so that you can set overall targets in your budget.

| Click on the Edit button and then the Supercategories option.

2 Click on the chosen category.   3 Click on a supercategory.

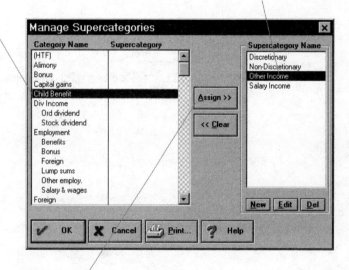

To deselect a category from its supercategory, click on the Clear button.

4 Click on the Assign button to assign the category to the highlighted supercategory.

5 Click OK when finished.

Moving around the Budget window

Using scroll boxes

To move quickly around the display you should make good use of the scroll bars.

To drag the right scroll box, click on it and hold down your left mouse button and then move up and down the scroll bar. A small window is displayed showing the item which will appear at the top of the list if you release the mouse button at that point.

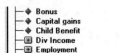
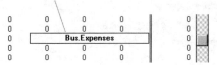

Using the keyboard

The following list of keys will help you move around the display with the use of the keyboard rather than the mouse. You can also use various keystroke combinations to move quickly to other parts of the Budget screen.

Tab or Right Arrow	Use these keys to move right, one column at a time.
Shift+Tab	Moves left one column.
Left Arrow	Moves left one column.
Enter or Down Arrow	Moves down one row in the same column.
Up Arrow	Moves up one row in the same column.
PageUp	Moves one screen up.
PageDown	Moves one screen down.
Home+Home	Moves to the first cell in the current row.
End+End	Moves to the last cell in the current row.
Ctrl+Home	Moves to the first row of figures.
Ctrl+End	Moves to the last row of figures.
Ctrl+Left Arrow	Scrolls display one page to the left.
Ctrl+Right Arrow	Scrolls display one page to the right.

Using the Progress Bar

Having set up your budget figures, you will need to compare them with the actual figures. Quicken does this very neatly with the Progress Bar.

The Progress Bar is displayed across the bottom of your screen, so that the options are readily available at any time.

From the Plan menu, click on the Progress Bar option.

The bar shows two slide gauges which compare the budget and actual figures up to the date specified.

Customising the Progress Bar

1 Click on the Customise button on the right side of the Progress Bar.

2 Click on the drop-down button and click on the budgetary type you want to display.

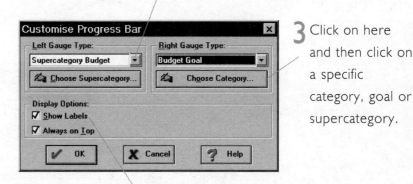

3 Click on here and then click on a specific category, goal or supercategory.

4 Click to display labels. Clicking on the box again removes the labels (category names) from above the slide gauges.

Savings Goals

This feature lets you 'hide' money for something you want to save for, such as a holiday, new kitchen, etc.. Although the money is really in your account, it is marked as being unavailable for other spending purposes.

Setting up a savings goal

1 From the Plan menu, click on the Savings Goals option.

2 In the Savings Goals window, click the New button.

3 Enter a name.

4 Enter the amount.

5 Enter the finishing date for the goal.

6 Select the currency you will be using.

7 Click OK to add the goal to the Savings Goals window.

Savings Goals window

Click on a savings goal to display its progress bar beneath it.

The progress bar displays the amount already 'put aside'.

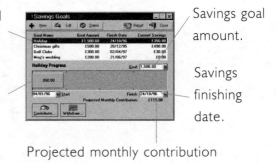

Savings goal amount.

Savings finishing date.

Projected monthly contribution required to meet the goal.

...contd

Contributing to your savings goal

1 Click on the Contribute button.

2 Enter the contribution date.

When the transfer has been added into the account a 'Hide Sav. Goal' checkbox will have been added at the bottom of the account register. Activating it will hide the transfer from the account.

3 Select the account to be used, from the drop-down list.

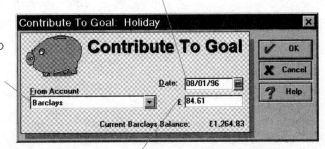

4 Enter the contribution amount. The predicted monthly contribution will be automatically entered but you can overwrite this if the amount to be set aside is different.

5 Click OK to finish.

Withdrawing from your savings goal

1 Click on the Withdraw button.

2 Enter in the transaction details.

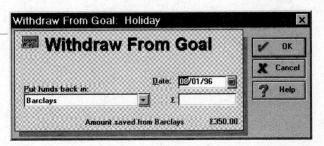

3 Click OK to finish.

Setting up a Loan

If you are thinking of getting a loan for some new equipment, an extension to the house or to see you through a sticky patch, Quicken can help you plan your loan.

Quicken can:

- Plan your loan in advance. If you know the interest rate to be charged, the program will work out the exact repayments over a given time.

- Allow you to check that the figures quoted by the Finance Company are correct.

- Continue to check your figures against the Finance Company's statements throughout the loan period.

To set up a loan in Quicken couldn't be easier. It asks you straightforward questions such as the total of the loan, the interest rate, the length of the loan, the Finance Company name, etc., and all of these are easily entered into the program.

The View Loans Window

To access the View Loans window quickly, press Ctrl+H.

From the Activities menu, click on the Loans option.

Select the loan you require, from the drop down list.

If you are entering your first loan, the details areas will be blank.

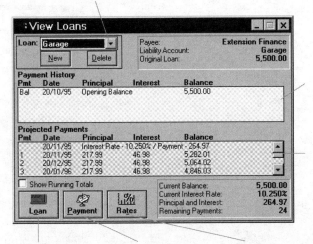

Panel showing repayments you have made on the loan.

Predicted payments including interest and balances.

Click to edit loan details in the Set Up Loan window.

Click to edit payment details in the Set Up Loan Payment window.

Click to edit rates details in the Loan Rate Changes window.

Entering Loan Details

Having committed yourself to a loan, you will want to enter the details into Quicken.

1 From the View Loans window, click on the New button.

2 Specify the loan type.

3 Specify if it is a new account or an existing one.

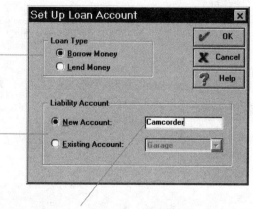

4 Enter a name if it is a new account.

5 Click OK to proceed.

Be sure to enter the correct dates. The first repayment may be on a future date and not the date of entry.

6 Enter the loan details.

7 Enter the number of payments to be made in a year.

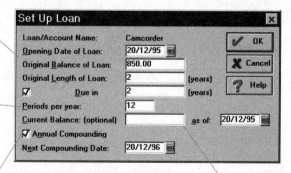

8 Click here, if the loan interest is recalculated annually.

When setting up a new loan account leave the Current Balance option blank.

9 Click OK to proceed.

10 Enter the interest rate. Quicken will automatically enter the principal and interest payment.

HANDY TIP

If you want to write cheques for the payment, click on the 'Chq' option from the drop down list.

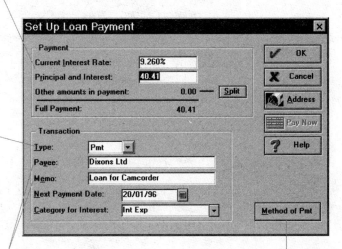

11 Enter the Finance Company name, an optional memo and an address if payment is to be made by cheque.

12 Select if the method of payment is to be a memorised or a scheduled transaction, and to enter the account from which it is to be paid.

13 Click OK.

The details will be displayed in the View Loans window and will be continually updated during the period of the loan.

REMEMBER

Loan details can be changed with the Loan, Payments & Rates buttons.

Double-click on the entry in the Payment History panel to access its account register.

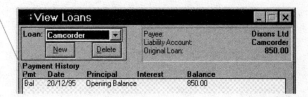

Paying Loans

When entering details of your new loan you should have defined your method of transaction. This is normally by memorised or scheduled transactions. You might have also instructed Quicken to give you a certain number of days notice of the due payment.

On the payment date, you will see the loan repayment being made into the appropriate account register.

If you have defined the loan payments to be paid by bank standing order or direct debit, then no further action needs to be taken, other than reconciling the entry with the next bank statement.

However, if you have decided to make payments by cheque, then Quicken's print cheque facility will store the information and, will prompt you to print the cheque.

If you are making payments by cheque, the account register will show the repayment transaction as 'Print' in the cheque number column, until the cheque is actually printed.

CHAPTER NINE

Financial Planners

Quicken can help make planning for your future easier. It offers financial planners for college, retirement, remortgage, as well as loans and savings, and it will help you to calculate how these will affect your finances in years to come.

Covers

Financial Planners.. 118

Planning your Savings Investment 119

Planning your Loan 120

Planning College Fees 122

Planning for your Retirement 123

Planning a Remortgage... 124

Financial Planners

From time to time it is necessary to look forward financially and plan for a future occasion.

When Quicken uses the word 'planning' it doesn't mean putting money aside, say for a holiday or some other special occasion. Planning as far as this chapter is concerned, is for much bigger occasions, such as those which relate to specific times in our lives.

Accessing the financial planners

1 Click on the Plan menu, from the Menu bar.

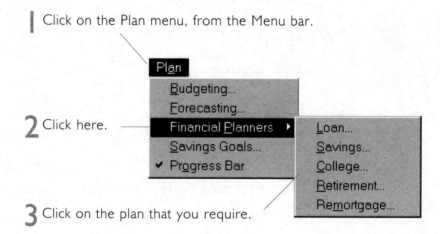

2 Click here.

3 Click on the plan that you require.

Planning your Savings Investment

With this planner, you can plan the growth of your savings. You will need to know a starting amount for your savings and what your regular contributions will be.

1 From the Plan menu, click on the Financial Planners option and then the Savings option.

2 Enter the amount you have already saved.

7 Click here to list the predicted savings and balances.

3 Enter the predicted interest rate.

Investment Savings Planner

Savings Information

Opening Savings Balance	50.00
Annual Yield	6.850%
Number of	Months	60
Contribution Each	Month	60.00
Ending Savings Balance	3,959.87

Schedule...

Done

Help

Calculate
- Opening Savings Balance
- Regular Contribution
- ● Ending Savings Balance

Inflation
Predicted Inflation 3.500%
☑ Inflate Contributions
☑ Ending Balance in Today's Money

4 Enter how frequently you are going to save, the number of contributions, and the amount to be saved each time.

5 Select if you want to display the expected opening balance or regular and ending balances.

6 If you are saving money over a long period, it is more than likely that the inflation rate will vary during that time. Quicken has included a number of Inflation options to help you calculate how it will affect your investment.

Planning your Loan

With this planner you can calculate loan amounts and loan payments for a given period of time. Obviously you need to have some details of the proposed loan so that Quicken can calculate the figures.

As an example, you could work out how much a loan for a car would cost, if paid over a given number of months or years, and at a fixed interest rate.

1 From the Plan menu, click on the Financial Planners option and then Loans.

Use the tab key to move quickly between entries.

2 Enter the amount of the proposed loan.

3 Enter the interest rate.

4 Enter the number of years and the number of repayments each year.

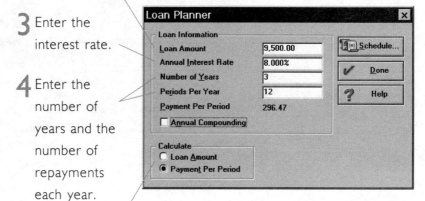

5 Use this option to specify whether you want to see loan details or the repayment amounts.

6 Click the Schedule button, to open the Approximate Future Payment Schedule window.

Approximate Future Payment Schedule

This window displays a table of payments based on the information you have just entered.

 Use the Page Up and Page Down keys on your keyboard to move around the schedule.

 There are a number of formulas used to produce the results of such a table. You can therefore reasonably expect the figures shown in the listing to differ, by a few pence, from the amounts that will be shown on the Finance Company's statement.

Click here if you want to print the payment schedule.

Column showing how much goes towards paying off the loan.

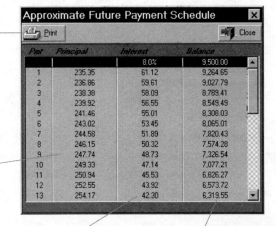

Column showing the amount going towards the interest.

Column showing what the loan balance will be after you make a payment.

Planning College Fees

If you have children and want to give them a private education, this is the planning feature which will help you do the long term financial planning for it.

You will need to know the number of years until enrolment, the number of school years, the estimated annual fees, any current savings, and the amount you can afford to contribute towards the fees.

 Each child's school fees have to be calculated separately.

1 From the Plan menu, click on the Financial Planners option and then the College option.

2 Enter the expected annual college fees, the number of years before the child will enrol and the number of years expected to attend there.

6 Click here to display a list of predicted savings and balances.

 You can also use this feature if you want to go back to education.

3 If you already have some savings for this purpose, you can include them in your calculations.

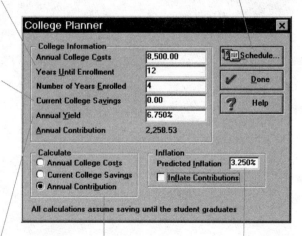

College Planner

College Information
Annual College Costs	8,500.00
Years Until Enrollment	12
Number of Years Enrolled	4
Current College Savings	0.00
Annual Yield	6.750%
Annual Contribution	2,258.53

Schedule...

Done

Help

Calculate
- Annual College Costs
- Current College Savings
- Annual Contribution

Inflation
Predicted Inflation 3.250%
Inflate Contributions

All calculations assume saving until the student graduates

4 Enter an average expected interest rate for the period.

7 Enter the predicted inflation rate.

5 These options let you calculate what tuition you can afford, the amount you should have already saved and how much you need to save each year.

Planning for your Retirement

REMEMBER **If you have more than one retirement account, you must make separate calculations for each.**

With this planner, you are able to perform 'what-if' calculations to plan for your retirement. For these calculations you need to know, or guess at, the interest rate over the period, current age, retirement age, the withdraw until age, and any other income.

To calculate how much money you need to start your retirement plan:

1 From the Plan menu, click on the Financial Planners option and then the Retirement option.

2 Enter the required details in the Retirement Information section.

7 Click here to view the list of deposits you must make to achieve your retirement goal.

3 If your retirement account is tax-free then click on Tax-Sheltered Investment.

4 Check that the current tax rate is correct.

REMEMBER **Interest rates may change over a long period and may produce different end figures.**

5 These options let you calculate the amount required to start off the investment, the amount you need to save each year and how much you will have during your retirement years.

6 Enter any adjustments required to allow for inflation. This item is optional.

Planning a Remortgage

With this financial planning calculator, you can determine whether it is to your best advantage to refinance a mortgage. A lower interest rate doesn't always mean refinancing is the best step to take. You will also have to take into consideration any fees, closing costs, and other charges which may have to be made.

1 From the Plan menu, click on the Financial Planners option and then the Remortgage option.

2 If you enter the current payment and annual compounding, the program will calculate the principal/interest amount.

3 Enter the principal amount, years, interest rate and click on annual compounding. Quicken will calculate the monthly principal/interest amount and the monthly savings.

Remortgage Planner

Existing Mortgage
Current payment: 240.00
monthly principal/int = 240.00

Proposed Mortgage
Principal amount: 15,400.00
Years: 25
Interest rate: 8.250%
☑ Annual Compounding
monthly principal/int = 122.80
monthly savings = 117.20

Break Even Analysis
Remortgage closing costs: 250.00
total closing costs = 250.00
months to break even = 2.13

Done
Print
Help

4 If you enter the remortgage closing costs, the program will calculate the total closing costs and the months to break even.

5 Click on the Done button when finished.

CHAPTER TEN

Shares & Investments

With the advent of privatisation a lot of people have, as a result, become shareholders. Quicken will help you to keep track of your shares and will show whether you are making or losing money from them.

This chapter will take you through each stage of using Quicken to keep track of your investments.

Covers

Adding an Investment Account 126

Setting up Securities 128

Setting up Security Types 129

Setting up Investment Goals 130

Setting up Security Balances 132

The Investment Account Register 133

Buying 134

Selling 135

The Portfolio View window 136

Adding an Investment Account

There are three things to be done when setting up a shares investment account. Firstly you must set up the account (see below), secondly enter the securities in that account (see Setting up Securities), and finally enter the initial number and value of the shares for each security in the account (see Setting up Security Balances). Quicken lets you track more than just one security in your shares investment accounts.

1 From the Activities menu, click on the Create New Account option and then click on the Investment button.

2 Enter the name of your investment/share account.

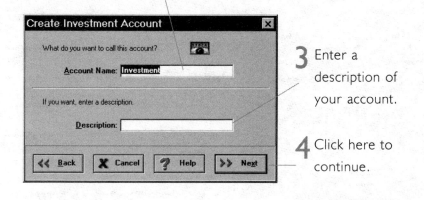

3 Enter a description of your account.

4 Click here to continue.

5 Select the currency type.

6 Select whether or not it is to be a PEP account.

...contd

BEWARE

Once set up as a shares investment account it cannot later be changed to a unit/investment trust account.

7 Click on the No button if you are going to track it as a normal shares investment account rather than a unit/investment trust account.

8 Click on the Done button.

Quicken will ask you if you want to add the Portfolio view icon to the main iconbar, but only if it is the first investment account that has been set up.

Click on here and the icon will appear on the iconbar.

Clicking here will give you access to the Portfolio View window.

Quicken will now open the account register and you will now be able to create the securities for this account.

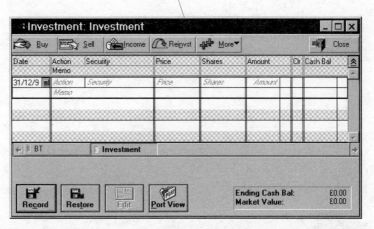

Setting up Securities

Quicken defines Securities as a single investment that has a value and usually a share price. Typical securities are -shares, bonds, gilts, unit/investment trust, a fixed term deposit or a property investment trust, and can also be a collectable or precious metal.

To access the security list, press Ctrl+Y.

1 From the Lists menu, click on the Security option.

2 Click on the New button.

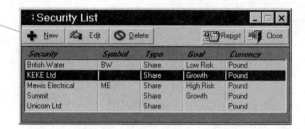

3 Enter the security name.

4 If you plan to import price data from an ASCII file, enter a symbol, e.g. 'TT'.

Go to the Setting up Security Types section, if you want to customise the security type list, and the Investment Goals section if you want to customise the goals list.

5 Select the security type and goal, from their drop down lists.

6 Select the security currency.

7 If the security is a tax-free security, click here. Tax-free securities are filtered out of capital gains reports.

8 Enter the amount you expect to earn annually.

9 Click on the OK button, and your new security will be listed in the Security List window.

Setting up Security Types

Probably the best way to list security types is in the order they are listed in your daily newspaper. Look in the listing for the share price for the new security you are creating, and note the name of the group where it appears. Add that group if it does not appear in Quicken's default listing.

Quicken needs to know the security types for reporting purposes, so it is necessary to specify a security type for each of your securities. The program allows you to have up to 15 different security types.

As you use the Portfolio View, you will see that Quicken sorts securities by type. The program also lets you create investment reports that group securities by security type.

1 From the Lists menu, click on the Security Type option.

2 Click on the New button.

3 Enter the security type.

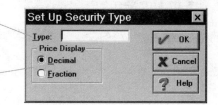

4 Select the way you need to view the prices.

Editing and deleting the security type is performed in the same way as for securities.

5 Click OK to finish.

Setting up Investment Goals

It is a good habit to have a goal for a security, so that you can see your securities by goal, printed in investment reports. Look on this facility as an open option to include a reference to your investments.

You can define your goals in many ways. One unusual but useful way is using it to remember who suggested to you to purchase the security, so that a broker, friend or relative can be entered as the goal. Then you can create a report showing you who gave the best advice.

Making use of goals will allow you to group and analyse your investments by goals whether they are in the same account or different accounts.

Displaying the Investment Goal List

From the Lists menu, click on the Investment Goal option.

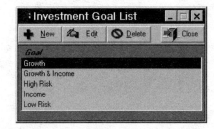

Adding a new goal

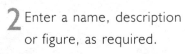

1 Click on the New button.

2 Enter a name, description or figure, as required.

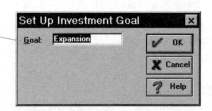

3 Click OK, and it will be added to the list of other goals.

...contd

Editing a goal

⎮ Click on the Edit button.

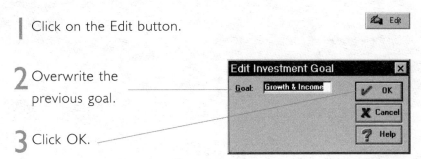

2 Overwrite the
previous goal.

3 Click OK.

Deleting a goal

⎮ Click on the entry to
be deleted.

2 Click the Delete button.

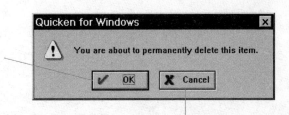

3 Click OK, to
confirm the
deletion.

Click here to abort the procedure.

10. Shares & Investments **131**

Setting up Security Balances

It is a good idea to enter into Quicken the details of the initial purchase or acquisition for each security. This information can be entered in either the investment register or the Portfolio View windows.

1 From the Accounts list, double-click on your new investment account to open it.

2 From the register buttonbar, click on the More button.

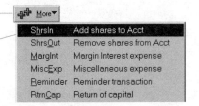

3 Click here.

4 Enter the date.

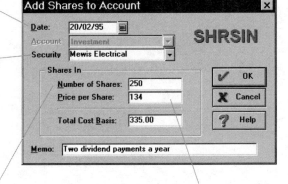

REMEMBER

If you need to set up the security see Setting up Securities, (earlier in this chapter).

5 Select the security name from the drop-down list.

HANDY TIP

If you enter a value for the Total Cost Basis, but leave the Price per Share box empty, Quicken will calculate the price per share and enter it into the box.

6 Enter the number of shares purchasd on the date shown in the date box.

7 Enter the initial share price, which should be in pence in the UK.

8 Enter the total cost, which will include the total cost of the shares plus any extra fees such as commission.

9 Enter a meaningful memo about the shares.

10 Click OK. The transaction will then appear in the account register.

The Investment Account Register

REMEMBER

Fluctuations in the share prices cannot be counted as being transactions.

The Investment Account Register looks slightly different from the other account registers in that the column headings are different.

You can enter and record all of your share transactions here, including buying and selling, reinvesting dividends and recording income.

1 From the Accounts list, double-click on your investment account to open it.

REMEMBER

You may have to set up a security (see Setting up Securities section).

2 Enter the date.

3 Enter the action (e.g. buy, sell, reinvest etc.).

4 Select the security.

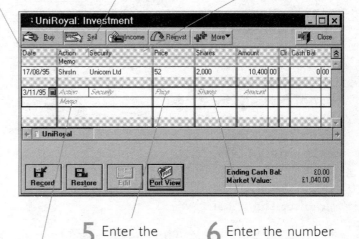

HANDY TIP

Quicken calculates the total value of your shares automatically.

5 Enter the share price.

6 Enter the number of shares.

7 Enter a meaningful memo about the transaction.

8 Click on the Record button.

Instead of entering transactions directly into the register it may be easier to enter them in the relevant transaction windows, by clicking on the Buy, Sell, Income, Reinvst and More buttons displayed in both the register and Portfolio View window.

Buying

1 From the accounts register or the Portfolio View window, click on the Buy button.

2 Enter the transaction's date.

3 Select the security name, from the drop-down list.

4 Enter number of shares bought.

When you press the tab key (on your keyboard) after entering the number of shares and price, Quicken will automatically calculate the total cost of buying the shares. Any extra commission/fee costs entered will also be automatically added to the total.

5 Enter the share price, and any other costs and fees.

Buy Shares

Date:	08/01/96
Account	UniRoyal
Security	Summit

BUY

Cost
Number of Shares: 5.000   Lots...
Price: 15.550
Commission/Fee: 25.00

Total of Purchase: 802.50

✓ OK
✗ Cancel
? Help

Transfer Acct: [Haifax]   [Optional]
Amount to transfer: 802.5
Memo:

6 Select the account from which you will pay for the shares, and amount removed from it.

7 You may want to enter a memo about the transaction.

8 When complete, click OK.

The entry will then be displayed in the register.

Select the transaction and click on the Edit button if you want to change any of the details in this window, or simply edit the details directly in the register.

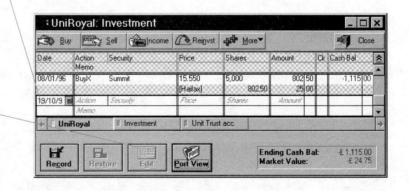

Selling

1 From the accounts register or the Portfolio View window, click on the Sell button.

2 Enter the transaction's date.

3 Select the security name, from the drop-down list.

4 Enter number of shares sold.

5 Enter the selling price, and any other costs and fees.

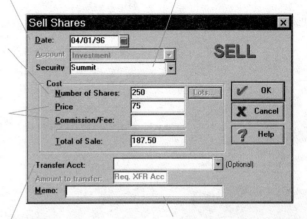

6 Select a transfer account if you intend to place the money into another account, or you can leave the money in the investment account.

7 You may want to enter a memo about the transaction.

8 When complete, click OK.

The entry will then be displayed in the register.

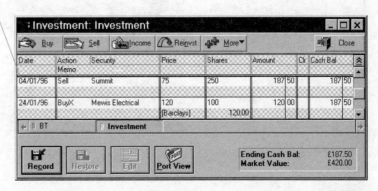

The Portfolio View window

The Portfolio View window lists all the securities in the selected account, and displays the number of shares you have, their current market price and their market value performance.

It is most important if you have shares and investments, that you keep abreast of current values and trends, so that purchases and sales can be made at the best times.

In the Portfolio View window you can enter investment transactions, change the security prices, and create graphs showing the value and price history for a particular security.

Accessing the Portfolio View window

HANDY TIP The Portfolio View option can also be selected by pressing Ctrl+U.

From the Activities menu, click on the Portfolio View option, or from the Investment register click on the Portfolio View button.

Using the Portfolio View window

These buttons are the same as those in the Investment Register.

Click on the More button to display other transactions, and then click on the option you require.

HANDY TIP Actual or estimate gains (or losses) are shown at the bottom of the columns, with the percentage gain (or loss) displayed in the panel underneath.

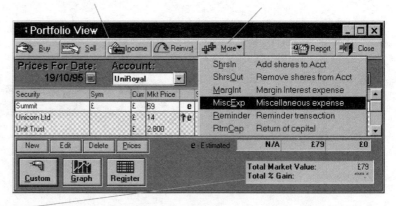

The control view options

Below the Portfolio buttonbar are four control view options.

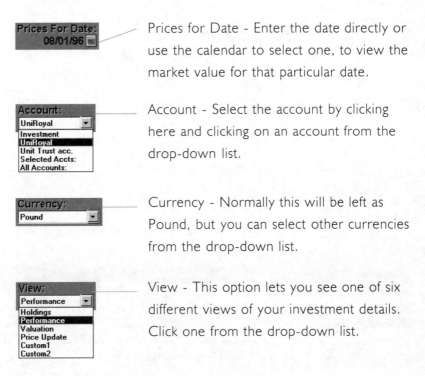

Prices for Date - Enter the date directly or use the calendar to select one, to view the market value for that particular date.

Account - Select the account by clicking here and clicking on an account from the drop-down list.

Currency - Normally this will be left as Pound, but you can select other currencies from the drop-down list.

View - This option lets you see one of six different views of your investment details. Click one from the drop-down list.

Producing reports

Move your mouse pointer over a security name so that the pointer changes to the QuickZoom magnifying glass, then double-click and a report for that entry will be displayed.

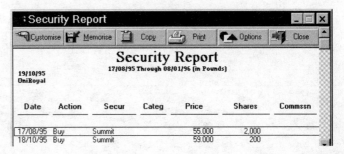

Other Portfolio View buttons

Clicking on the Custom button allows you to customise the Portfolio View window.

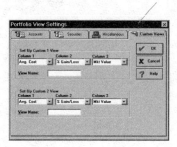

Clicking on the Graph button will display a graphical view of price history trends for a selected security.

REMEMBER

To produce investment graphs see the Investment Graphs section in Chapter 6.

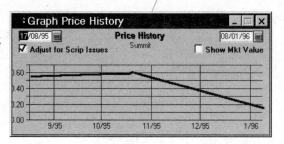

Clicking on the Register button will send you back to the Investment register.

CHAPTER ELEVEN

File Functions

A Quicken file is basically a collection of accounts, which share the same categories, classes, currency list, memorised transactions and VAT control. Each file in turn is unrelated to any other Quicken file.

This chapter will explain how to create, delete and access your files, and how to back them up.

Covers

Adding a New File 140

Opening a File 141

Deleting a File 142

Backing Up Files 143

Restoring Backed Up Files 144

Setting up Passwords 145

Copying Details to the Next Year 146

Adding a New File

Most people will only need one file when they first start using Quicken but in time you may need to create new files, for example to keep your business and home finances in different files, or to keep each year's accounts separate.

1 From the File menu, click on the New option.

2 Click OK. Quicken will have the New File option selected by default.

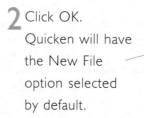
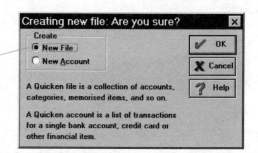

3 Enter the file name. It can be up to eight characters long.

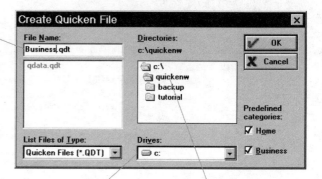

4 Select the drive you want the file to be stored in, from the drop-down list.

5 Double-click on the directory you want the file assigned to.

6 Click on the Home and Business checkboxes if they are not already activated.

7 Click OK. The new file will be created with the Create New Account window already opened.

Opening a File

When you have more than one file in Quicken, the program will always go to the file you were last working in when you start it. It is, however, quite easy for you to access your other files.

To access the Open Quicken File window quickly, press Ctrl+O.

| From the File menu, click on the Open option.

2 Enter the file name here, making sure not to delete the .QDT extension.

or

By double-clicking on the file name you will open the file without having to click on the OK button.

2 Click on the chosen file, so that it appears in the file name box.

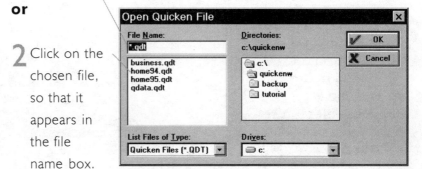

3 Click OK. Quicken will automatically close the last file (including the window) you were last working in and open the new file.

Deleting a File

Deleting your files should be done with caution as you will not be able to get that file's account data back.

Deleted files are not recoverable, and there will be no record of it in Quicken.

1 From the File menu, click on the File Operations option.

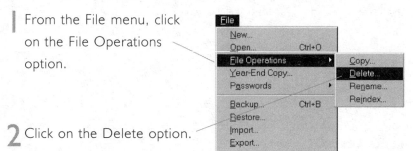

2 Click on the Delete option.

It is a good idea to backup the data on the file you are about to delete, just in case you need it in future.

3 Click on the file you want to delete so that its name appears in the File Name box.

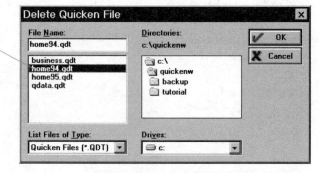

By double-clicking on the file name you will go straight into the Deleting File window without having to click on the OK button.

4 Type in YES to confirm the deletion.

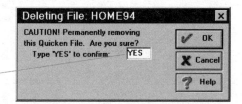

5 Click OK.

Backing up Files

The Backup option records the data file produced in Quicken, for extra security. Without this protection, should your computer hard disk fail, you will lose for ever all the entries you made.

If you have a dedicated backup program, the Quicken backup function may not be of interest to you. If however you don't, then Quicken back up is very easy to use.

 It is important to backup your files at regular intervals. Quicken will periodically prompt you to backup the data files when you leave the program. This is normally set for each third time you use the program.

1 Place a formatted floppy disk in the disk drive.

2 From the File menu, click on the Backup option.

3 Select Current Files if you are backing up your working file, or click on Select From List for the file list.

4 Select the drive you require from the drop-down list.

When complete, label and clearly mark the floppy disk and keep it in a safe place, away from the computer, or other similar electrical equipment.

5 From the list, click on the file name to be backed up, so that it appears in the top box.

6 Click here.

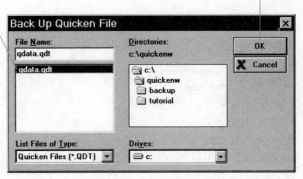

7 After Quicken has told you that the backup is complete, click OK and remove your backup disk.

Restoring Backed up Files

So your computer has crashed, the hard disk has decided to call it a day, or just your Quicken data file has become corrupted. Any of these can and do happen, usually without warning. Whatever the reason, you will be glad you made a backup of your data file, and now you will need to restore it.

1 Place the floppy disk, containing the backup files, into your disk drive.

2 From the File menu, click on the Restore option.

3 Click on the drive containing the backup disk, from the drop-down list.

4 Click on the name of the file to be restored.

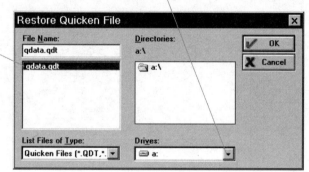

5 Click OK.

REMEMBER

Your backup file may not contain the last entries you made before the computer crashed, or got corrupted.

6 A window may be displayed asking if you want to overwrite the existing data file. If that file is in some way corrupted, click on the Yes button, and the backed up file will be restored.

7 Click OK and remove your backup disk after Quicken has told you that the file has been restored.

Setting up Passwords

There are two levels of password protection - files and transactions. Selecting files will prohibit anyone without the password looking at your Quicken data. Selecting passwords on transactions will allow someone· else to enter transaction but not view previous entries.

Don't make your passwords too obvious or difficult to remember.

To set up your password

1 Open the file to be protected with a password.

2 From the File menu, click on the Password option and then click on either File or Transaction.

Write down your passwords and store them safely. It is also a good idea to change your passwords regularly.

3 Enter the password. It can be up to 16 characters. Uppercase and lowercase characters are treated the same. Then click OK.

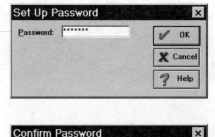

4 Confirm the password and click on OK.

Your file can still be copied, deleted or renamed even with a password, but your password will always remain linked with the file.

To set up passwords on transactions follow the above procedure, but at Step 3 you will see this window.

3 Enter your password and a date to define 'previous' entries.

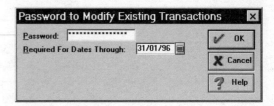

Copying Details to the Next Year

After running Quicken for a while you will have all the settings and configurations just to your liking. It would be a pity, and time consuming, to go through the setting up procedure every year.

To save you the trouble, Quicken has a little feature which makes a copy of your current year's file, and then removes all transactions from it, without altering or destroying the original. You end up with a file which is ready to accept transactions, together with all the settings used in the previous year.

1 From the File menu, click on the Year-End Copy option.

2 Click on the Start New Year option.

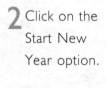
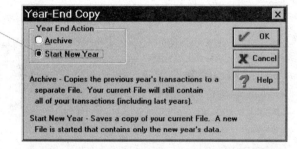

3 Click OK.

4 Enter a new name for next year's file.

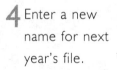
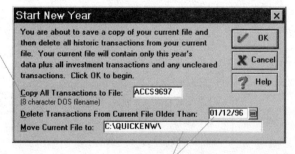

5 You can delete transactions prior to a specified date. You can also move your current files to a different directory.

6 Click OK. Finally the File Copied Successfully window will be displayed. Click on the checkbox of the file you want to access next.

CHAPTER TWELVE

Miscellaneous Features

This chapter includes other Quicken features which you will find useful when it comes to dealing with multi-currency transactions.

Also covered, if you are going to use Quicken for business use, are the VAT related features.

Covers

Currency 148

Selecting International Preferences.......................... 150

Using the Calculator 151

Tracking VAT 152

Changing VAT Rates 154

Currency

The chances are that you will only be using one currency in Quicken and that will be the Sterling Pound.

However, if you have a secret bank account in Switzerland, receive an income from an apartment block in Spain, or manage great Aunt Hilda's finances in Australia, the program can cater for such situations.

Quicken's currency list displays all the foreign currencies that it currently recognises. Quicken allows you to add or delete currencies as required.

Accessing the currency list

From the List menu, click on the Currency option.

If you want to print the currency list, press Ctrl+P.

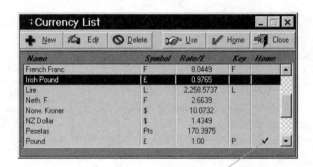

As standard for the UK version, a tick will be shown against Pound, as this is the home currency.

Click to add a new currency to the list.

Click to delete the highlighted currency.

Click to change the home currency to the currency highlighted in the list.

Before deleting a currency make sure that it is not being used in a register.

Click to edit the highlighted currency.

This option selects a currency for an amount entered in a register.

Editing a currency

This facility is useful when you want to edit a currency to match the current rate of exchange.

| From the Currency List, click on the currency to be edited, and then click on the Edit button.

You can use short-cut letters for your currencies, which can speed up the entry of foreign currencies in the registers.

2 Enter the new currency exchange rate. Only one figure needs to be entered as Quicken will calculate the other.

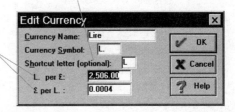

3 Click OK.

Changing the home currency

| From the Currency List, click on the currency, and then click on the Home button.

Only change the home currency during a financial year if absolutely necessary, as it may upset your existing transactions.

2 You will be asked to confirm that you want to change the home currency. If you do, click OK.

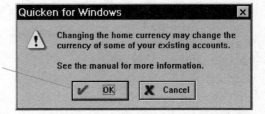

Selecting International Preferences

If you are going to use multi-currency transactions you will have to change some of the International Options settings. These will already be set up for use in the UK, if you have bought your Quicken program in the UK.

1 From the main iconbar, click on the Options icon, and then click on the International button.

HANDY TIP

Although Quickens options are already set up for the UK and Australia you can customise Quicken so that it can be used anywhere in the world.

2 Click on the country setting.

3 Select the Cost Basis Calculation.

4 Select the amount you want share prices to be adjusted by, in the Update Prices and Market Value screens.

5 Select this checkbox to display the currency units in terms of 100ths, e.g. $1 is shown as 100.

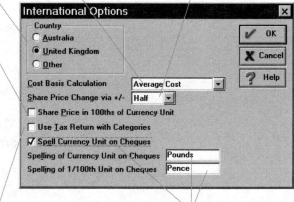

BEWARE

Changing the Country option will automatically reset the options to their default settings for that country - these options can be altered, if necessary.

6 Select this checkbox if you want to feature tax returns with categories.

7 Select if you want to spell out the chosen currency in your cheques. Then enter the spelling of the currency units.

8 Click OK to finish.

Using the Calculator

Once the calculator is selected it remains on top of Quicken or any other Windows program you may switch to. This means that calculations can be made from details in one program, and then pasted into Quicken.

Surprisingly little is said about the calculator in the Quicken manual or Help screens. Quicken's pop-up calculator can be more useful than it appears at first sight.

Activating the calculator

From the Activities menu, click on the Use Calculator option.

This calculator has the facility of memory recall, unlike the small drop-down calculators from the amount fields in the transaction registers.

It can be used from either your keyboard or by clicking on the figures and operations with your mouse pointer.

You can paste results from the calculator directly into various amount fields in the Quicken program by clicking on this button.

Tracking VAT

If you are in business and are VAT registered, you will need to keep track of all your VAT payments and receipts in order to produce quarterly (sometimes monthly) VAT reports.

When you first installed Quicken and defined your accounts, or when you added new accounts, an option during the process asked if you wanted to 'Track VAT'.

Click here if you want to track your VAT.

If you answered 'Yes' to this question, Quicken will automatically produce an account called 'VAT Control'.

It is advisable to review existing codes to make sure that the VAT rates are correct for your business.

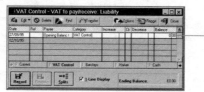

This account keeps a running total of the VAT payable (or refundable).

This account can also be opened from the Accounts List:

1 Click on the Accounts icon on the main iconbar.

2 Click on the Other or All Types tabs and double click on the VAT Control account.

Alternatively click on the VAT Control button in the main accounts bar from the register window.

...contd

Switching on VAT Tracking

If your VAT status has changed since you opened your account you can change it quite easily:

1 From the main iconbar, click on the Accounts icon to display the Accounts List.

2 Click on the account to be changed.

3 Click on the Edit button.

4 Click the Track VAT option.

5 Click OK to finish.

REMEMBER

If you used Quicken's preset list of business categories when you created your data file, the categories will already have VAT codes assigned to them.

Defining the VAT rate

You also have to define the VAT rate for each category.

1 From the List menu, click the Category and Transfer option.

2 Click on the category which is to be assigned a VAT code and then click the Edit category button.

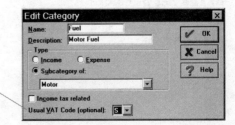

3 Click on the Usual VAT Code drop-down list and select a VAT code.

Changing VAT Rates

Quicken easily keeps track of VAT on your income and expenses, however the current rates have to be entered. It could well be that the rates haven't changed since the last version of Quicken was written, in which case changing the settings may not be necessary.

To change the settings

From the Lists menu, click on the VAT table option.

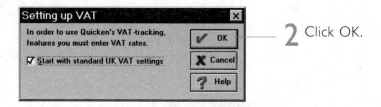

2 Click OK.

The first two rates, Exempt and Zero-rated, are both shown as having a zero percentage, while the Standard rate has 17.50% already entered.

The Edit VAT Rates window allows for 10 rates to be entered.

The first three are the rates most often used.

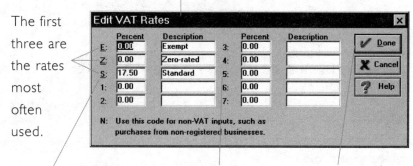

Percent refers to the percentage of the net price of goods that has to be paid as VAT.

Quicken uses the VAT code, either a letter or number, instead of showing the percentage rate in full.

If there are other rates which apply to your business, enter them against the remaining numbers.

3 Click here, when you have finished.

Index

A

Accounts
adding 24 - 26
adjusting the balance 94
balancing 90
deleting 27
reconciling 89
transferring between 33

B

Backing up files 143
Balancing accounts 90
Bank statements, reconciling 92 - 94
Billminder 58
Bonds. *See* Securities
Budgets 102
figures
duplicating 104
entering existing data 105
exporting 105
manually entering 104
Progress Bar 109
supercategories 107
window
tidying up 106
viewing 103

C

Calculator 151
Cash accounts
updating balance 100
Categories 13, 23
adding 28
deleting 30
recategorising 31
splitting 29
subcategories 28

Category & Transfer list 28, 30
CD-ROM version 22
Cheques 61
aligning 65
making a credit card payment 99
making loan payments 116
options 63
printer setup 64
printing 59, 66
writing 62
Classes 23
adding 32
subclasses 32
Colours, register 34
Credit cards
payment 99
reconciling 98
writing cheques 99
Currency 26, 148
adding 148
editing 149
home currency 149
international preferences 150
list 148
updating exchange rates 149
Customising
graphs 82
reports 68

D

Direct debits 42, 52, 116. *See also* Scheduled transactions
Drop-down lists 21

F

Files 23, 139
adding 140
backing up 143
deleting 142

opening 141
passwords 145
restoring backed up files 144
year-end copy 146
Financial Calendar 49
automatically adding transactions 21
buttons 51
customising 50
notes 60
opening 50
options 51
scheduling a transaction 54
Financial planners 117
Finding
and replacing 48
text and figures 48
transactions 46
transfers 47
Fixed term deposit. *See* Securities

G

Gilts. *See* Securities
Graphs 73. *See also* Snapshots
accessing memorised graphs 84
budget 76
creating 74
customising 82
income and expense 80
investments 78
memorising 84
net worth 81
options 75
printer setup 83
printing 83
QuickZoom 77
security's price 138

H

Help
icon 22
menu 22
QCards 17

I

Iconbar 14 - 16
adding icons 15
customising 14
editing an icon 16
removing icons 15
International preferences 150
Investment goals
deleting 131
editing 131
setting up 130
Investments 125
adding an account
setting up securities 128
setting up security balances 132
setting up the account 126
buying 134
performance graphs 78
portfolio 136
reconciling 96
register 133
selling 135
unit trust accounts
reconciliation 95
unit/investment trust account 127

L

Lists
account 26, 36
category & transfer 28, 30
class 32
currency 148
icon 15
investment goals 130
memorised transactions 42, 51
scheduled transactions 52
securities 128
security type 129
standing orders 52
Loans
entering details 114
paying 116
planner 120

setting up 112
window
   predicted payments panel 113
   repayments panel 113

M

Memorised transactions 42
  calendar 51
  list 42
  loans 116
Memorising
  graphs 84
  reports 72
  transactions 42
Multimedia tutors 22

N

New User Setup 10 - 13

P

Passwords 145
Paying
  bills 40
    in advance 57
  loans 116
Portfolio graphs 78
Portfolio View 97
  customising 138
  window 136
Precious metal. *See* Securities
Printer setup
  changing font settings 64
  cheques 64
  graphs 83
  reports 70
Printing
  cheques 66
    from Reminders window 59
  graphs 83
  preview 71
  reports 71
Progress Bar 109
Property investment trust. *See* Securities

Q

QCards 17
Quick Keys 18
QuickFill 20, 39, 43, 51
  options 21
QuickZoom
  graphs 77
  reports 68
  Snapshots 85
  to reports from graphs 77

R

Recategorising 31
Reconciling 89
  accounts 91
  bank statements 92 - 94
  credit card statements 98
  investment accounts 96
  unit trust accounts 95
Register 26, 35
  1-Line Display 36
  changing colours 34
  configuring 20, 38
  entering payments 40
  investments 127, 133
  opening 36
  options
    display 38
    miscellaneous 39
    QuickFill 20
  reports 41
Reminders 59
Remortgage planner 124
Reports 61, 67
  accessing memorised reports 72
  creating 67
  customising 68
  memorising 72
  options 69
  printer setup 70
  printing 71
  securities 137
Retirement planner 123

S

Savings goals 110
  contributing 111
  setting up 110
  withdrawing 111
Scheduled transactions 52 - 54
  adding 53
  assigning a payment date 54
  deleting 56
  editing 55
  grouping 53
  list 52
  loans 116
  paying in advance 57
Securities 128
  adding the opening balance 132
  graphs 138
  investment goals 130
  list 128
  portfolio 136
  reports 137
  setting up 128
Security balances 132
Security types
  list 129
  setting up 129
Share accounts
  updating balance 100
Shares 125. *See also* Investments
  adding an account 126
  adding the opening balance 132
  buying 134
  portfolio 136
  register 133
  securities 128
  selling 135
Snapshot pages
  adding 88
  customising 86
  deleting 88
  editing 88
Snapshots 85
  customising 87
  QuickZoom 85
SpeedKeys 16

Splitting categories 29
Standing orders 42, 116. *See also* Scheduled transactions
Starting Quicken 9
Subcategories 28
Supercategories 107

T

Talking Tutorials 22
Targets. *See* Budgets
Transactions
  adding 37
  deleting 44
  entering 35
  finding 46
  memorised 21
  memorising
    automatically 43
    manually 42
  scheduled 52 - 54
  voiding 45
Transfers
  finding 47

U

Unit/investment trusts. *See also* Securities
  adding an account 127
  reconciling 95

V

VAT
  category VAT codes 28
  changing VAT rates 154
  defining VAT rates 153
  splitting category VAT rates 29
  tracking 25, 152
Voiding transactions 45

W

Writing cheques 62